The Spur Master Guide to Snow Camping

Other titles in this series include:

Ski Touring (Master Guide) by Rob Hunter
Outdoor Skills (Master Guide) by Brown & Hunter

Venture Guides

Outdoor First Aid
Weather Lore
Map & Compass
Basic Skiing
Backpacking
Hill Trekking
Survival & Rescue
Lightweight Camping
Winter Camping
Cross Country Skiing
Parallel Skiing
Walking
Camping & Backpacking Cookbook
Youth Hostelling

A complete list of titles may be obtained from
Spurbooks Limited, 6 Parade Court, Bourne End, Buckinghamshire

The Spur Master Guide to

Snow Camping

CAMERON MCNEISH

SPURBOOKS LIMITED

Published by
Spurbooks Limited
6 Parade Court,
Bourne End,
Buckinghamshire

Acknowledgements

The publishers would like to thank the following people for their help in preparing this title: Rob Hunter; John Traynor of 'Camping' magazine. Peter Lumley of 'Camping World'; Jack Jenson for Canadian information; Berghaus Ltd, Newcastle on Tyne; Terry Brown for the illustrations; John Rae & Tony Lack of Pindisports for technical advice; Estelle Huxley.

British Library Cataloguing in Publication Data
McNeish, Cameron
The Spur master guide to snow camping.
— (Spurbooks master guides).
1. Snow camping
I. Title II. Master guide to snow camping
796.54 GV198.9

ISBN 0-904978-42-7

Designed and Produced by
Mechanick Exercises, London

Printed in Great Britain by
Galbraith King & Co. Ltd, London

Contents

Publisher's Introduction

ABOUT THIS SERIES

This book, a Master Guide to Snow Camping, is one of a new advanced series, designed as a follow up to the well-known and successful Spurbook *Venture Guide* series for beginners.

Master Guides are not for beginners. They are for people who already have a year or two of experience in their chosen activity and wish to develop it *or* they cover activities which, by their very nature, are not for beginners. Master Guides will cover Cross Country Ski Touring; Ski Mountaineering; Advanced Rock Climbing; Lond Distance Walking; Expeditions; Outdoor Skills; and, the subject of this book, Snow Camping. Other titles will follow.

ABOUT THIS BOOK

With the introduction of better equipment, and a good grasp of summer or three-season techniques, many campers and backpackers now want to extend their activities into the winter. However, winter in the hills can be a different matter altogether from the same place in summer, and the presence of snow puts every activity and item of gear under fresh scrutiny. In this book, Cameron McNeish covers the entire area of snow camping, from equipment to technique, on how to start and how to develop snow camping skills in safety and enjoyment.

ABOUT THE AUTHOR

Cameron McNeish, who lives at Aviemore in the Highlands of Scotland, is an experienced backpacker. He writes regularly on the outdoors for many magazines, and tests equipment for leading manufacturers. This is his third book.

1 · Making a Start

Welcome to the world of winter, to those cold, clear mornings when your breath is suspended in the air, when the trees bow their branches under a new mantle of snow, when your footsteps crunch loudly in the silence of the snowfields.

Inside the tent the warm comfort of the sleeping bag is left for the start of the day's activity. The cold air nips and hurries you through the usual chores of breakfast, striking the tent and packing, and once on the trail, the blood pulses through the veins and the beauty of the hills makes the heart beat faster.

This, in brief, is the attraction of winter. It is the time of year when the wilderness becomes wilderness again. The eroded tracks and the tin cans of summer have disappeared beneath the snow, and even familiar places look fresh and different.

The ultimate experience in walking, camping or backpacking is to live and travel in winter, for days on end, on foot or on skis, wandering further and further into the snow covered hills.

It is, of course, possible to enjoy the winter world on day trips, but to fully enjoy the experience, and to get really into the wild, longer stays become necessary, for it is only by living in the snow that you can fully enjoy the relationship which exists between the camper and the winter environment. This is a relationship which will, for a while, seem cold and distant, but growing experience will eventually allow you some familiarity, and it will become fun.

So, after gaining some summer experience, accept the challenge of winter's frozen gauntlet. Here you will have a chance to participate in an extreme form of camping, a form which requires skills, knowledge and strength, both physical and mental, which are not often required during the lazy days of summer. Almost anyone can camp during the summer, and in these overcrowded days it sometimes seems as though everybody is! Winter is the true backpacker's season, the season which tests your gear, skill and capabilities to the full.

There are some basic skills which must be learned before the camper even sets foot in the winter backcountry. There is gear to acquire, skills to master, experience to gain. These elements in combination will keep you secure in the winter, and these are the elements you will find in this book.

BEFORE YOU START

There is no doubt that more and more campers, especially lightweight campers and backpackers, are continuing their activities right through the year, but it must also be obvious that camping in winter, especially under snow conditions, can be completely different from the (sometimes) summer sun-kissed version. Competent, experienced, summer campers can make the transition to winter without too much difficulty; different skills are learned, and progression is gradually made until he or she is as happy in the snow as they would be camping on a warm summer meadow.

Having said this, *newcomers* to camping and backpacking, would be well advised to *first gain a fair amount of experience walking and camping in the relative comfort of summer.* Snow camping is not the sort of sport which you suddenly just take up! It requires a summer, or better still, a *three-season* apprenticeship; a mastery of those techniques and skills which will allow you to live in safety and comparative comfort in the wilds in summer, autumn and spring. Once this target is achieved then it becomes a natural move to extend the season into winter and acquire those techniques as well. Before you even think about *camping* in the snow, it is, I believe, important to gain some experience just *walking* in snow. As you will discover in the forthcoming chapters, winter provides her own challenges and even dangers. You will need to be alert to counter them at all times, and you must be aware of the actions and skills which have to be employed to avoid them.

A few one-day trips will give you some idea of the problems and pleasures of winter.

WINTER SKILLS

Before you strike out into the winter wilds:-

1. Familiarise yourself with different types of snow conditions.
2. Learn how to use an ice axe and crampons.
3. Read as much as you can about snow and avalanches.
4. Know the symptoms and treatment for exposure.
5. Learn how to dress yourself to keep the icy fingers of winter at bay.

Before you even *consider* camping on snow you should be familiar with:-

i. Navigation (the use of map and compass).
ii. Weather forecasting.
iii. First Aid.
iv. Basic campcraft.

Snow camping is an extension of skilful summer activities. If you lack these basic skills you will find yourself in an uncomfortable, if not dangerous situation in the winter hills.

This book is a Master Guide, and Master Guides are not for beginners, but for those who already have a basic grasp of some particular outdoor activity. To save continual reference to basics, it will be assumed that the reader already possesses such basic skills. If not, they can be studied in the *Master Guide to Outdoor Skills,* also published in this series, or in any one of the Spurbook Venture Guide series.

GETTING STARTED

As an experienced summer camper or backpacker you will probably already own a fair amount of equipment, much of which is perfectly suitable for winter work. We will go into the additional gear more fully in a later chapter, but for the present let us take a look at the kit which you will require for a trip in snow conditions.

COMPLETE KIT LIST

The following list should cover everything which may be needed for any winter trips, from the simple requirements of a one day walk in the mountains to the full equipment required for winter camping in snow. You may not need all of it all the time, but you will need some of it sometime.

* = possible group items.

Items required for day trips:
Underwear. Wool or *Lifa* (or similar)
Shirt (wool)
Wool or thick *Helenca* breeches or trousers
Sweater or fibre pile jacket
Socks — two pairs
Insulated parka or windproof jacket
Boots with cleated sole
Mittens or gloves with spares
Woolly hat or balaclava
Goggles or dark glasses
Watch
*Map (1:50,000 minimum scale, 1:25,000 is better)
*Compass
*Food, plus emergency food
*First Aid Kit
Emergency 'bivvy bag'
Rucksack
Whistle
Matches
Candle
Paper/pencil
Pocket knife
Torch (with spare batteries) or Head Lamp
Gaiters.

If going *anywhere near hills,* the following should also be taken:-

Ice axe
Crampons (10 point)
Avalanche cord/sonde (bleeper)
*Flare

Overnight Gear:
*Tent, strong enough to withstand winter weather
Sleeping bag
Insulation pad
Eating gear
*Stove
*Fuel for stove
*Pots
Mug
*Water carrier
*Plenty of matches in waterproof container/lighters
*Candles
*Plastic bags (useful for various purposes)
P. Bottle (marked 'non-potable')
*Altimeter
Tent clothes/spare clothes/down bootees
Personal hygiene requisites
A good book and/or a small radio

HOOD WITH
WIRED VISOR
JACKET WITH ZIP
AND VELCRO FASTENING
OVERTROUSERS
WITH LEG ZIPS
KNEE LENGTH GAITERS

Optional:
*Sunburn cream/lip salve
*Snow saw and shovel
*Ski waxes and torch/aerosol sprays
Skis/poles/boots
Camera and film
*Rope 9mm (kernmantle)

*Those items marked with an asterisk are usually shared items.

Specialist items, like ice axes and crampons can usually be hired until you decide that snow travel is for you. Always check hired equipment carefully for wear or damage. You can also use three-season gear in winter with a few additions. Extra sweaters and socks can be used in place of specialist down clothing, and your 'three-seasons' sleeping bag can be modified for winter use by placing a thinner one inside it, or sleeping with your clothes on. Many summer tents can be made usable in winter by sewing on additional guy ropes and pegging points, but unless you have a proper bona-fide winter tent, your pitch must be well sheltered and safe, and it would be inadvisable to camp too high.

I have never been an advocate of the *'practice your first pitch in the back yard'* school. This gives a totally false sense of security, especially in winter. It is better to find an experienced partner, and ask him (or her) to take you along on the next trip. In this way you will learn from someone else's experience, which is much quicker than by feeling your own way. Better still, join a course in winter hillcraft or winter backpacking. The outdoor journals carry advertisments from suitable schools and centres and these courses will give you all the basic knowledge and a modicum of practical experience.

After one or two trips you will feel confident enough to head off into the hills with companions of similar experience, and this is where the fun and the learning really begins.

WINTER CAMPING ACTIVITIES

Of all outdoor people, it is probably the backpacker who gains most from snow camping. The backpacker can extend his season outside the summer months, so much so that, in many cases, winter becomes the true backpacking season, leaving the milder weather available for canoeing, sailing, walking, windsurfing, or some other pastime. Family men and women will enjoy taking the children out in easy conditions during the summer and leave the harsher weather of winter for their own trips.

Photographers can also gain much from snow camping. In winter the countryside is at its most beautiful, pristine and clear, without the usual haze of summer. In the wilderness and backcountry astonishing landscapes appear, just asking to be photographed. In the cities snow quickly becomes dirty and slushy, certainly not a photogenic subject, but in the wilds, nature can be captured at its very best.

Cross-country skiing and ski-touring are becoming popular sports. There are basically, two types of cross country skier. The outdoors person who wants additional range for his winter backpacking trips may learn to ski on Nordic skis, and moving easily and fast over the snow can eat up the distance without wading through deep snow. The experienced alpine, or downhill, skier, fed up with queuing at chairlifts or tows, and who wants to enjoy his skiing far from the 'madding crowds' will find ski touring

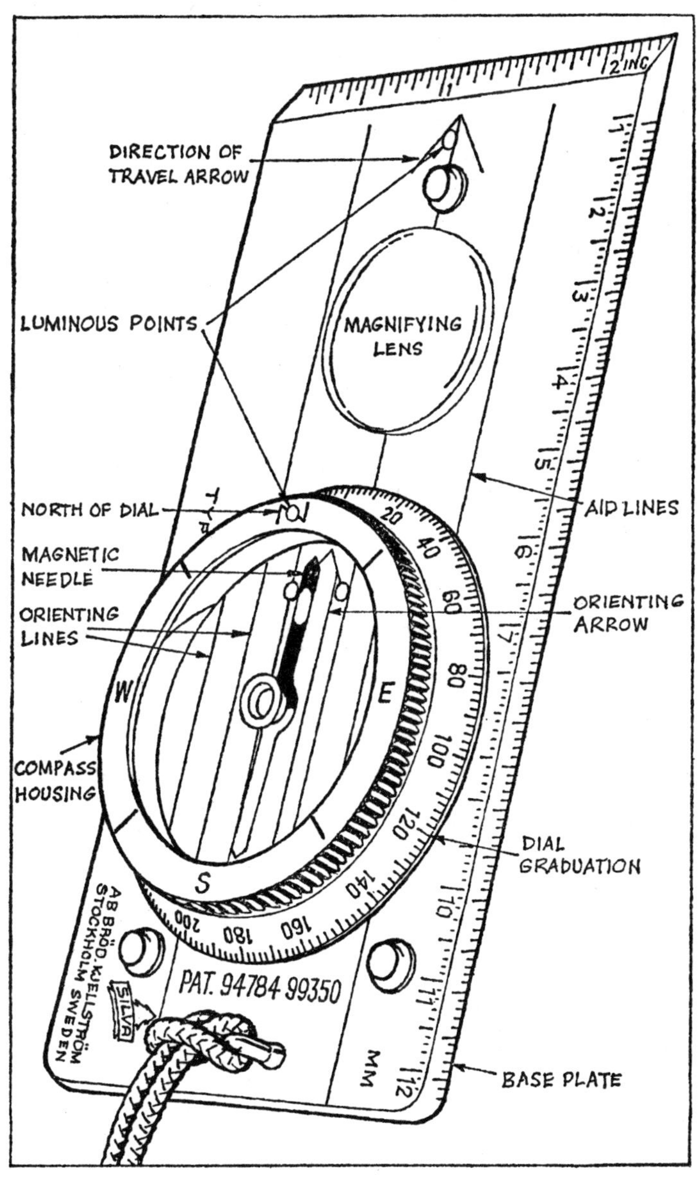

The Silva compass

fascinating. Whether you use skinny Nordic skis or heavier 'mountaineering' skis, there is no doubt that your pleasure can be increased by camping out at night, which allows you to wander over the snowfields at will without having to return completely to a hotel or hostel base.

Apart from such enthusiasts, those who simply enjoy camping should know how to camp all the year round, and not feel obliged to pack their gear away when the leaves fall, and wait out the months until spring.

WEATHER

Before we go any further, I want to raise the subject of weather. You *must* have a good understanding of weather — indeed, the most important winter skill needed by the snow camper is the ability to read the weather. All the hopes and plans for coming trips, for continuing the journey, and how high in the hills we can afford to go are dependent on the signs, or absence of signs of coming storms. Wind, rain, slight snow showers, mist, overcast days, or even the sun melting the snow crust can and should cause alterations to clothing, timings, or routes. Mix some of these bad ingredients together and the result often means digging in deep until the weather improves, or getting right out of the hills altogether. You have to be very tough, experienced and lucky to beat the winter on its own ground.

FORECASTS

It does, of course, help enormously to listen carefully to the weather forecasts (and understand them) before you leave home. Papers, radio, television, or the local meteorological office found on most airfields, can offer up forecasts of varying exactitude. Don't fail to get a forecast. If you ignore a bad forecast you may regret it. Take the weather into account, plan a different route, perhaps a more sheltered one, and when you do head into the hills, make doubly sure that you have also planned good and reliable *escape routes,* all along your chosen trail. Do this always, as a routine, not just now and again, but as a habit.

As an experienced *summer* outdoors person you should already possess a basic knowledge of meteorology, and can at least identify different cloud formations and what weather they are likely to bring. If not, start learning now, for weather lore is a basic outdoor skill, one to be acquired early. David Unwin's *'Mountain Weather for Climbers'* is excellent, as is the Spurbook Venture Guide to *'Weather Lore'.*

Even with basic weather knowledge, never neglect to use your eyes. Be weather conscious, ask *locally* about *local* conditions, and above all, use your common sense. If you get reliable information regarding the weather, don't ignore it; if the forecast is bad — act accordingly, plan an easier route, or go home. The hills will still be there next week.

DEVELOPING SNOW CAMPING EXPERIENCE

Only when you feel fairly competent in moving about in the wilds in winter has the time come for the first overnight trip. The best way to do this is to find someone who is already experienced in the winter and who is willing to take you along.

The first-hand teaching situation is the finest possible way to learn the differences between summer and winter campng. A companion is a valuable asset in winter, and although I have many times argued about the advantages of solo backpacking in summer, come the long dark nights and cold short days of winter and I go with a companion, if only as an important part of the safety kit.

The experienced man knows how to avoid these dangers, what to look for, and if necessary how to get out of bad situations should they arise. A companion who is a winter beginner like yourself, will not be of too much help, and if you are sensible you will both be limited in the early days to easy ground where there are no real dangers. In any event, let your experience grow with your ability and develop naturally.

You will need to acquire some extra clothing and gear, just to stay warm and move about. Some you may have already, or it may be possible to adapt it. Either way, let us now look at clothing and equipment.

2 · Clothing

Camping and backpacking, even in high summer, can often be a damp and chilly experience, but it is the winter months which bring together the harsh realities of wind, wet, and cold. A combination of these three elements has a marked effect upon the human body, and what might merely be an unpleasant experience in summer, could easily have a tragic finality in winter unless you have the proper clothing and equipment. In addition to the different climatic conditions, we must also consider the problems of walking on snow, and perhaps ice, for much of the day. In mountainous country, where a slip could lead to a long, fast slide, an ice axe and crampons become important items of equipment, the essential hardwear of the winter walker. Add to these problems the aggression of a winter storm, shorter days, and poor visibility, and it becomes obvious that proper clothing, good technique and a grasp of the essential skills will play a much more important role in winter than they would in the halcyon days of summer.

CLOTHING LIST

Select from the following and wear as necessary:

Lifa or woollen underwear. T-shirt, vest, and long-johns.
Woollen or thick cotton shirt, preferably with chest pockets for keeping odds and ends.
Two or three thin sweaters for insulation. (Two or three thin ones are better than one thick one).
Wool, Orlon, or *Helenca* breeches or trousers with hip pockets and front pockets.
Two pairs of socks. (If there is any rubbing in your boots it is better to have the rubbing between the two socks rather than sock and foot).
Insoles. Plastic latticed ones give more insulation and last longer.
Boots with *Vibram* soles, sealed against the wet.
Fibre-pile jacket.
Down filled or polyester filled Parka with pockets, hood, and flapped zip front.
Rain jacket and rain trousers, (also doubles effectively as wind-suit).
Mitts or gloves.
Wool hat or preferably balaclava.
Gaiters. Calf length to prevent socks from becoming wet or to prevent snow from entering the top of the boots.

Additional Items:
Waterproof mitts.
Overboots (Down bootees).
Down filled suit.
Facemask.

Spare Clothing: To be carried in the pack in a waterproof bag and kept dry at all times.
Socks — as many pairs as possible.
Spare underwear.
Polar suit or spare sweater and long-johns.
Hat or neck-cloth or dry bandana.
Slippers — for nocturnal excursions.

CLOTHING

Comfort and protection, rather than appearance, are the keynotes of functional outdoor clothing. Let's take comfort first. If we don't feel comfortable day after day on the trail, it won't be long before discontent steps in, and that certainly will not increase your enjoyment of the outdoors. Comfort in clothing means light weight and adequate ventilation. The ease with which such garments can be put on or taken off in the limited space of tent or snow hole is also a factor. Warmth, with wind protection, are the important points. All garments *must* offer protection to the body.

Protection means exactly what it says; protection from the elements. The winter camper and walker has to stop the body being affected by extremes of wet and cold, separately or in combination. The garment must also help to prevent excessive heat loss for the human body is not capable of handling low temperatures by itself and stopping excessive heat loss calls for one thing; *insulation.* Insulation is usually proportional to garment thickness, that thickness being the amount of material necessary to trap air effectively. This trapped or 'dead air' is then warmed by heat from the body. Insulation also prevents body warmth being lost by convection, that is by the action of air blowing over the body surface which carries away the warm air and replaces it with cold.

Insulation can be gained in two ways. The first is by using a thick garment, like a down-filled duvet or a thick fibre-pile jacket which, with good breeches and underwear will trap the air in the filling of the pile, or between the garments. The alternative is to wear a system of layers, for several thin garments will trap air between their layers. If necessary, and in extreme conditions, both these methods can and should be used simultaneously.

LAYER CLOTHING

The 'layer' concept for clothing is a sound one. Let us start next to the skin, with underwear. Wool, or a good wool blend, is excellent. It doesn't get wet easily, it dries well and it often serves as a 'wick' and draws moisture away from the body. Wool retains its heat-trapping qualities even when wet, unlike other materials which simply break down into a sodden mass when damp.

Unfortunately for some people, wool also means irritation when worn next to the skin, especially on the arms and legs, so for comfort an alternative must be found. I use and therefore recommend Helly Hansen Super *'Lifa'* underwear. This polypropylene material passes the body moisture out along the fibres and into the next layer of clothing, keeping the all important layer next to the skin warm and dry. Two days of hard walking seems to be the limit with *Lifa* before the body salts clog up the pores of the material and make it less effective, but a wash-out even in cold water restores the warm qualities and it dries out in next to no time. *Lifa* comes in roll-neck tops, in T-shirt tops with long or short sleeves, and pants or 'Long-Johns'.

A good alternative to *Lifa* is the traditional Norwegian fishnet underwear which helps to keep you cool in the summer and yet well insulated in winter, by trapping warmed air in the open weave. If you try fishnet underwear, make sure you get the type with ordinary close woven material in the shoulders, or the straps of your pack will force the netting into your shoulders. The same is true of the hip area, where the belt of your rucksack is positioned.

Some people swear by 'Long-Johns', some people swear at them; it's a matter of personal choice. I tend to belong to the pro-'Long-John' fraternity, providing the garment is of a stretchy type material. I have used, with great success a pair of stretch ballet tights. They are comfortable, light, not in the least bulky, and most important, warm. When you consider that a fair amount of the body's heat is lost through the thighs, then it may well be worth seriously considering the value of long-johns or tights.

SHIRTS

The next layer consists of some type of shirt, trousers or breeches (knickers) and socks. Once again, wool shirts have amassed a great following throughout the years, and justifiably so. Wool/nylon mixtures are very popular because of the cost, while flannel shirts wear well and have most of the qualities of wool. Whichever type of shirt you wear, check that it has a long tail. Chest pockets are also useful. A bandana or scarf seals off the neck area quite nicely, and can come in handy for many other uses as well.

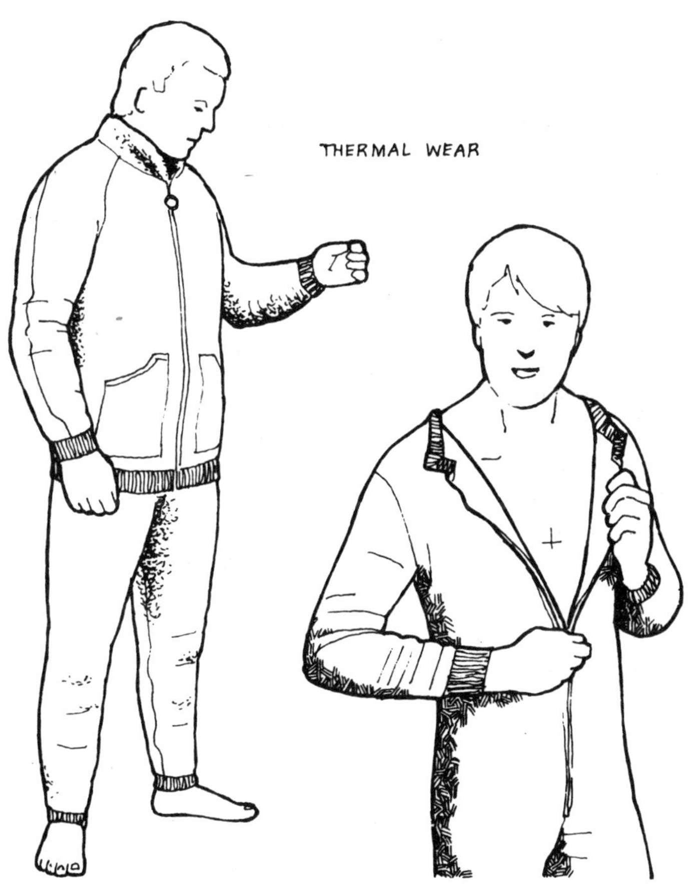

FIBRE-PILE

Two years ago I started wearing a fibre-pile jacket immediately over my underwear. The dense fibre-pile effectively traps the body-warmed air, and the full length zip down the front makes ventilation easy. A shirt is not always necessary, for a fibre-pile jacket, or a zipped woollen pullover usually provides all the insulation and warmth required, except in severe sub-zero conditions.

TROUSERS

Wool trousers or breeches have dominated outdoor wear for a good few years, but great strides have been made recently with the use of nylon. 'Helenca' stretch nylon fabric is now used in the manufacture of breeches, a 'spin-off' from the ski trade, which provides a warm, easy to dry, very comfortable, snow-shedding alternative to wool.

Whether you use breeches or trousers is very much a matter of personal choice, but try and find a pair which are self supporting, for trouser belts and rucksack hip belts are not truly compatible.

SALOPETTES

A bib and braces type garment called a *salopette* used mainly by cross country skiers, is also very functional for winter campers and ski tourers. The great advantage is that they eliminate the cold spot between the top of the trousers and the shirt which often occurs when you bend over or when the shirt rides up.

OUTER GARMENTS

Many backpackers like to wear two or three sweaters on top of their shirt. This is an excellent idea, for the insulating air is trapped between the layers, but problems arise when the body becomes overheated due to hard walking or climbing. The walker then has to stop, take off his pack, remove the required amount of sweaters, put them in his pack, and put the pack on again. A far better method is simply to wear a zipped fibre-pile or zipped wool sweater on top of the underwear, an insulated vest on top of that, and, if the weater is really cold, a 'parka' on top of the vest. A combination of vest *and* parka is quickly becoming more popular than the old idea of one thick duvet jacket, because the combination offers more options and ventilation. *Adjustability* is the name of the game. Every moment you spend on the trail something happens which will make you warmer or cooler. Struggling up a long slope, stopping for lunch, being caught in a sudden downpour, fighting into the teeth of a sudden gale, sunshine, temperature, your own personal metabolism, everything changes constantly. The body itself has various ways of adjusting to different temperatures, but these adjustments are limited. This is where a good system of clothing comes in. You are much better thinking in terms of one garment doing a single job, rather than buying something with *reputedly* does a few jobs in one garment. For example, a fibre-pile jacket for heat retention plus a windproof outer parka is better than one thick, heavy, windproof garment. The big heavy outer jacket is fine when it's cold at the halt, but what happens when you are sweating up a steep hillside with a forty pound pack? You have given yourself no choice and you will sweat heavily. The combination, or 'layer' system of garments allows you to put on or take off a layer or two to suit the conditions of the moment. Full length zips on all the layers make things even easier. When you are too warm, pull down the zips

HOODED CAGOULE

on all the layers and let the cool air in; too cold, pull the zips up again. This is simple, functional, easy to operate and so control ventilation, and these are the features to look for in all your outer garments. But . . . zips are potential cold spots. It is pointless having an expensive well-filled *"Thinsulite"* or down parka, if cold can enter through the zips. Zip flaps with press studs or velcro strips to close over them are essential, and you should not even consider buying a parka which does not have such a feature. Velcro will freeze in snow and become ineffective, so velcro *must* be covered.

Hand-warmer pockets, which are open pockets situated behind the main flapped pockets, are very useful, but in my experience, most of the parkas have these pockets placed directly on the spot which is covered by the rucksack hip belt. Nevertheless, it's better to have these hand warmer pockets than be without them, as during the periods when you are not wearing a pack or gloves you can slip your hands quickly and without thought into the pockets without having to undo flaps and unzip zippers.

Down-filled parkas are remarkably warm garments, almost as warm as the traditional duvet jacket. However, once the down becomes wet, through rain, mist or wet snow, it matts and loses most of its effectiveness. If you are likely to encounter conditions like this, and this will be the case in most parts of Europe and in the Eastern U.S.A., then a polyester-filled parka will be much more functional. Polyester, the current favourite, *Hollofil,* or *Thinsulite* have the ability to retain warmth even when sodden wet, retaining the loft to trap that dead air which in turn retains body heat.

HOODS

Hoods usually come as optional extras on parkas, but I would suggest that you pay the little extra cost and buy one. When the wind blows strong and cold an insulated hood is a great boon. The head gives off a great amount of body heat, and if the neck and ears feel cold, then your whole body will feel cold. A wool hat or balaclava will keep the head warm, but if there is any naked space at all around the neck or head, then the cold will find it. Removable hoods are also useful if you have a sleeping bag that is not fitted with a hood, or a non-mummy-shaped bag. With the sleeping bag tied up around the neck, and the parka hood covering your head, neck and ears, you have an excellent alternative to a full mummy-shaped bag and fitted hood.

SHELL CLOTHING

Quite often the prime clothing consideration on the winter trail is stopping rain from entering. Should you get wet in winter the resulting chill and steady dampness can have drastic effects on the body. Once the body comes into contact with wet clothes, heat loss by *conduction* takes place. Water conducts heat away from the body up to 240 times faster than still dry air, so a person dressed in wet clothing when the temperature is low may lose heat just as fast as if he were immersed in cold water!

Besides this direct cooling effect, wind and water rob certain types of insulation of all their effectiveness. Down-filled garments are virtually useless when wet, which, in damp climates helps to explain the popularity of synthetic fillings such as *Hollofil* or *Thinsulite.* This is where good shell clothing plays its part. Until recently, sealing yourself up in a polyurethene or neoprene-coated nylon cagoule meant that you soon became wet inside from condensation. This was a warm wetness and better than being wet-cold, but it was still unpleasant. The advent of *Gore-Tex* material has reduced this problem and garments in this material are becoming increasingly popular with outdoor people. The microporous make-up of *Gore-Tex* allows body heat vapour to escape to the outside air, but stops rainwater droplets from entering. More and more walkers are using *Gore-Tex* now. The major disadvantage of *Gore-Tex* is that in order to be effective the material must be scrupulously clean. Being comprised of billions of tiny holes, big enough to let body vapour out yet too small to let rain water in, body salts and oils will soon clog the material. A quick wash every couple of weeks or so soon restores the breathing qualities of the material, so I would recommend *Gore-Tex* garments to all snow campers.

HEAD-PROTECTION

It is said that up to 60% of the body's heat is lost through the head. Therefore a woollen hat or balaclava is an indispensable item for winter wear. Use one which can be pulled down over the ears, like the balaclava, which can also protect the neck. In extreme conditions of cold and in the wind, a face-mask makes a useful addition to the kit, for cold wind will chap the lips and flay your face. A good barrier cream is also useful.

Whatever you wear on the head, make sure it can be worn comfortably in conjunction with the hood of your parka. In wet cold weather, don't be afraid to zip up completely in your shell suit, with the hood pulled well up over your head. A nylon or *Gore-Tex* hood does not offer a great deal of protection without the added insurance of a wool hat.

MITTS

Mittens are warmer than gloves, because the fingers can touch each other and so keep warm. *Dachstein* woollen mitts are excellent value and will last many years. They keep your hands warm even when soaked through, something which is quite likely to happen in the snow. Overmitts are also useful. These are usually made from nylon, and the better ones will have a leather palm. Silk inner gloves are good for extreme conditions, not so much for the added warmth they give inside the mitt, but as a protection to the hands when the mitts are taken off. If your bare fingers have ever stuck to a frozen camera or tent pole you will know what I mean. If not then this is an experience to avoid! Since gloves get wet, a spare pair should be carried in the pack.

OVERTROUSERS

Protection for the legs is also important, and good water- and wind-proof trousers should be capable of being taken off and put on easily *over boots.* Long zips, with gussets, up the sides of the trousers is the ideal method. All closures in rainwear should be capable of adjustment by draw-strings, velcro or snaps. An elasticated closure, especially around the cuffs, means that your ability to control the air circulation is severely curtailed. It is also a good idea to buy your rainwear as large as possible. This allows room for extra ventilation and permits you to wear a lot of extra clothing underneath if the weather is really foul.

Ponchos or capes, are not very good in winter. Their insulating value is next to nothing, and they flap and blow about in a wind.

COLD FEET

This is a problem which most of us experience at some time. Cold or wet feet can make life pretty miserable. There are a few obvious causes of cold feet. The commonest is leaking boots. Water gets in, the socks get wet through and heat loss by conduction takes place. Contact with cold surfaces like snow, draws heat from your body, and if you get wet it's even worse. Heat loss by conduction also takes place when your boots are frozen, which can often occur overnight, unless you protect the boots inside the tent. The cold surface of the frozen boot will draw away the heat from your foot, even if you are wearing good socks, and moving in frozen boots is hard work.

Even with dry boots, the feet can still get wet. Sweat evaporation is the culprit in this case. Contrary to popular belief, you don't *have* to sweat for evaporation to occur. There is always an invisible perspiration escaping from the skin, and as the perspiration soaks through the socks it cools, and so begins to condense. The result is damp socks, further heat loss, and cold feet.

There is also a less obvious way to get cold feet. The moment the body starts to lose heat faster than it can produce it, a series of involuntary actions are initiated to reduce the heat loss. The blood supply to the hands and feet is reduced in an effort to retain heat near the vital organs and in the body. Even though the rest of your body is quite warm, your feet will be cold, and unless this heat loss is stopped, ill effects will follow. The body can sacrifice a hand or foot in order to keep the body 'core-heat' stable, at least for a while. The solution is obvious, like wearing extra clothing, putting on dry clothing, or simply wearing a hat during cold spells. It may seem crazy to suggest that wearing a hat can cure cold feet, but in some circumstances that is quite correct. The head is the body's radiator, so keep the head covered. In winter wear two pairs of socks, carry plenty of spares and keep the feet warm and dry — always!

SOCKS AND INSOLES

Despite the various makes and types of socks available nowadays, good quality woollen socks are hard to beat. Wool is resilient, absorbs sweat well, and will keep the feet reasonably warm even when wet. This is because the hairy surface of wool traps the air, even when wet. Dry wool has a good 'wicking' action, allowing perspiration and humidity to be transported away from the skin, leaving a reasonably dry inner surface. A pair of thick woollen socks with a thinner wool pair underneath is a good combination. Two pairs of socks reduce friction and help to stop blisters forming. I usually carry at least two spare pairs of socks on a trip, and change them around every day. Changing socks from the left foot to the right foot also helps. Always keep your socks as clean as possible. Dirty socks insulate poorly, absorb less sweat and increase the possibility of blisters.

Plastic boot inner-soles or *neoprene* liners, also help to increase insulation. When you are standing still, your body weight compresses the socks, more or less eliminating any insulation value they may have had. Cold quickly creeps through the highly conductive sole of your boot and before you know what's happening, your toes are falling off with cold. Insoles help prevent this from happening, by trapping that all-important layer of still air. Latticed pattern insoles are particularly effective.

BOOTS

Good quality boots, big enough to be worn with two pairs of socks and still allow the toes to wriggle, are a *must* for winter hiking and camping, and certain features are essential in a well-made boot. Top grain leather has a natural resistance to water and is easily waterproofed. A minimum of seams is important as seams are a prime source of water entry, so go for a boot with as few seams as possible. A good overlapping closure and a sewn-in tongue is also important to keep the water out. Obviously, the more waterproof the boots are, then the greater risk there will be of body condensation forming inside, but this is where good socks come into their own. The boots should be dressed with *Sno-seal, Wet-prufe,* or *Nik-wax* at least once a season which will help keep the wet out.

GAITERS

As further protection against wet feet, a good pair of gaiters should be worn. Gaiters fill the space between boot tops and breeches and will prevent the socks or trousers from becoming wet. They also repel wind and provide an extra layer of insulation. They also change a pair of ordinary hiking boots into a pair of super *'wellies'* by sealing off the boot around the ankles and giving protection up to the knees.

So, to summarise what I have said about cold feet, remember, when your feet become cold, it does not necessarily mean that exposure or frostbite is around the corner, but it is simply nature's way of telling you that you are losing heat from somewhere faster than you are producing it.

SPECIALIST GEAR FOR EXTRA LOW TEMPERATURES

Down Bootees: These luxurious articles are useful to the backpacker as footwear to be worn in the tent at night, but in times of severe cold they can be worn *over* the boots with crampons fitted on the outside. They consist of ankle or calf high boots, in nylon, often with a suede side, with a down or polyester filling. The soles are usually made in suede, cordura nylon, or some type of non-slip material.

Face-masks: When the icy wind is blowing then it is not enough to just cover your head with a balaclava. Your face will need some type of protection from the wind as well. A balaclava, with holes for the eyes, is a good cheap form of face mask. It is also possible to buy special face-masks in deerskin which are excellent, but expensive, and not easily obtainable.

Down Suits: We have mentioned the use of down for parkas and its disadvantage in wet conditions, but in very cold, dry conditions, down is the best insulating material. A down filled suit, either a separate jacket and trousers, or an all-in-one suit, will keep you warm in intensely cold temperatures. Suits like this are worn by Himalayan climbers and some Alpinists, and are well suited to hanging about in bivouacs. They are used in some areas of the world for walking, although it is safe to say that most conditions experienced by the average backpacker would not be cold enough to warrant such a luxury. However, they are a deep winter garment, and in some Northern latitudes could be the answer to severe cold.

SPARE CLOTHING

In addition to the clothes which you wear from day to day, it is important to have something to change into at night in the shelter of the tent or snow hole, or wherever your night shelter will be. Winter nights are long, and to sit about for most of the evening in damp sweaty clothes will, at the very least, lead to a bad cold. You will also shiver the evening away, unable to warm up properly, and in winter you must stay warm.

Socks get damp very quickly during the course of a winter day, both from condensation and boot leakage. It is a good idea to change socks every day, but on an extended winter trip this could mean carrying very many pairs. If your socks cannot be clean though, let them be dry. In summer we can wash our socks as they become dirty, and dry them in the sun, but in winter it's not so easy. The best solution is to keep one pair dry in a 'poly-bag', using them only in the evenings. Down bootees can be used in place of tent socks but I find them a bit hot to wear for more than a couple of hours at a time. Unless they get wet, wear your outdoor socks for a couple of days at a time. Putting on damp socks in the morning is no fun and is the biggest deterrent to getting out of a sleeping bag that I know, but once you are out and about it's not so bad. Change the socks when they become really smelly or very wet. Three or four pairs is a good number to carry with you. Change them often.

UNDERWEAR

For reasons of hygiene, it's good to change your underwear fairly frequently. *Lifa* underwear only works well when fresh, for salt from the body clogs up the breathable pores. Two or three fresh sets usually suffices the length of a normal trip, and these suits weigh almost nothing and take up little room.

TENT WARM-WEAR

A *Helly Hansen* Polar suit lives in my pack all the year round. When the tent is pitched, and the sleepng bag lofted, I strip off my day clothes and put on the fresh, soft, luxurious Polar Suit. When the night is very cold I wear it in my sleeping bag, and it turns a good sleeping bag into an extra warm one.

Whatever you decide to wear in the tent, whether it's a Polar Suit, or just a spare sweater and Long-Johns, keep them fresh for night time wear. Don't be tempted to wear them during the day on the trail. Fresh dry clothing is a real moral booster at night, so don't sacrifice it for a change during the day.

SLIPPERS

Socks are usually sufficient for keeping the feet warm in the tent, but occasionally nature calls, or you have to go outside for more water or snow for melting. Instead of putting on wet or damp boots over your nice dry socks, it's a good idea to have a pair of waterproof slippers handy. Make sure they have a non-slip bottom though, or you will slip about on the snow like an ice skater. A few years ago I came across a pair of Norwegian wool slippers with a suede leather sole. The slipper was sock high and kept my feet very warm, and the suede leather sole allowed me to walk about in the snow without fear of slipping.

3 · Shelter and Sleeping

There is no doubt in my mind that short of a cabin, a refuge or a mountain hostel, which many people choose to use in the winter, the finest accommodation one can ask for when camping or walking during the winter months is a cosy, spacious, well-illuminated, properly designed tent. We will look at snow holes and emergency shelters later, but the basic item is the tent. A tent can be carried almost anywhere, pitched wherever the view is finest, and can be turned into instant accommodation at any time of the day or night. It is a true home for the winter wanderer *provided* the camper knows how to use it, and the tent is suitable for the climate and terrain.

The essential features of a winter tent are:

1. Stability.
2. Weather protection.
3. Strength.

For real *stability* I prefer the use of A-poles. For *protection* a two-skinned tent is best, although it must be borne in mind that in certain areas of the world, with very low temperatures, waterproofness is secondary to warmth. *Strength* requires the use of good quality materials, with absolutely no skimping on manufacturing standards. The emphasis should be on sturdy construction, with the inclusion of suitable design features, such as a snow valance to withstand the rigours of heavy rain and snow, strong winds, and any other nasties which the weather can and will throw at you.

WINTER TENT FEATURES

Features which should be included in a winter tent include:-

1. A large porch or bell-end for cooking and storing gear.
2. Two-skin construction, i.e., flysheet and inner tent.
3. A-pole construction for stability in wild weather.
4. A sewn-in groundsheet, preferably tray-shaped.
5. Extra pegging and guying points.
6. Reasonably light weight..

Let us now look at these features one at a time:-

Tent Shape: A winter tent should be large enough to allow you to bring *all* your gear inside. I do not like leaving my pack outside in winter at all, so a large porch is a necessity. A wind-resistant or wind-shedding tent shape is also advisable for wind is the real enemy of the snow camper.

Good quality tents are usually manufactured with what is called a *'catenary cut'.* This simply means that the panels and ridge lines are cut on the curve, so that the material, when stressed, can draw tight without wrinkling.

Pyramid-shaped tents are currently very popular among polar and high mountain expeditions, and have many practical advantages. The high

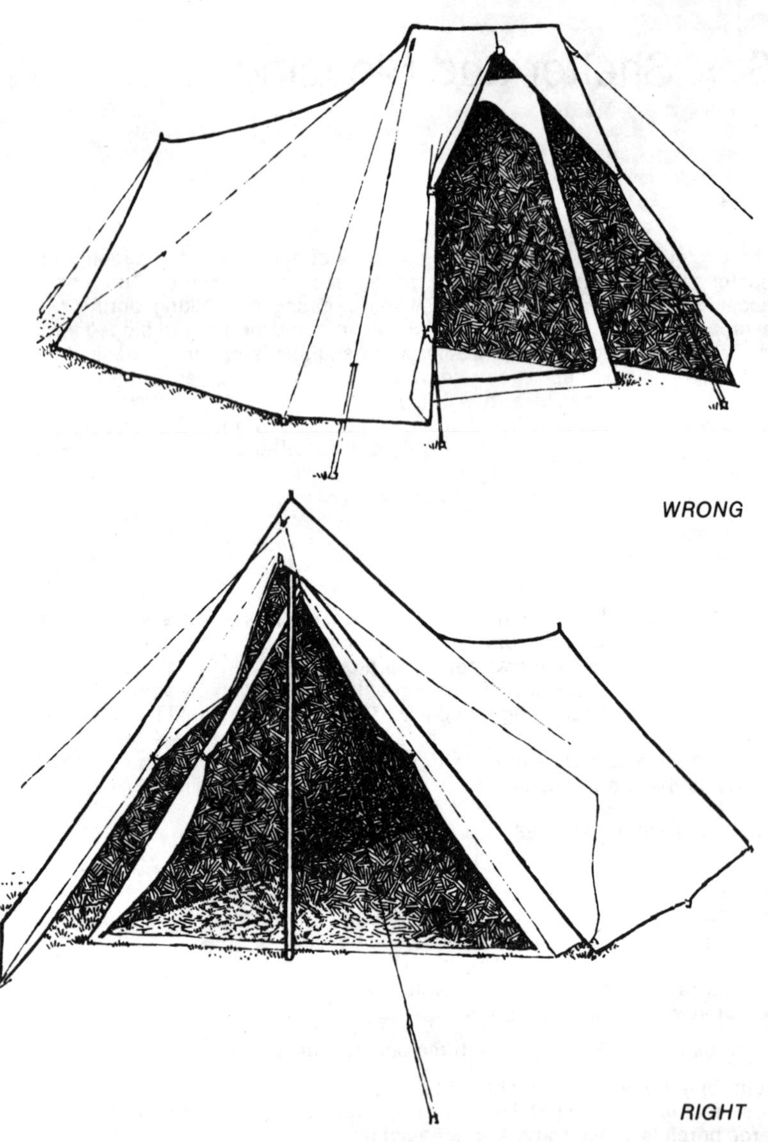

centre means that you can stand up inside. The pyramid shape spills wind well, and they are generally quick and easy to pitch. Those with a centre pole, rather than an A-pole, are not so useful for the centre pole, cuts down on usable interior space, so if you want a pyramid tent choose one with an A-pole.

Wedge-shaped tents, the ones with a square end and a sloping flat roof, have become very popular over the past few years, but I am still not convinced of their value as a winter tent. The square end certainly offers more elbow room, but the flat roof is a welcome sign to snow. Wet snow in particular, is very heavy stuff, and unless your tent is capable of shedding snow well, the weight of snow may collapse the tent, and certainly lead to heavy condensation on the inside.

Standard ridge tents, with A-poles at either end, a double porch on the fly, and sloping doors on the flysheet, are probably the best choice for ninety percent of snow campers. The A-poles give strength and security in rough weather, and allow the doorways to remain uncluttered. Double porches mean that you can use one end for cooking, and the other end for storing gear, and if you quarrel with your tent mate, one of you can live at one end while the other stays at the other! Best place for him!

In recent years, tunnel tents and hooped tents, equipped with fibreglass wands curved in an arch support, have become popular. They are being used a good deal for high mountain expeditions and this type of tent may well revolutionise winter tent design.

Weight: It is hard to generalise when talking about tent weight. Although we all aim for about three or four pounds (2 kilos) for a summer tent, a winter unit requires a bit more weight behind it to withstand the worst of a winter storm. The extra weight takes the form of heavier materials, A-poles, and bigger and heavier stakes and pegs. A two-man tent of around 6-8 lb (3-3.5 kilos) should be adequate for two, with possibly another couple of pounds (1 kilo) for a four-man tent. This weight can, of course, be shared among the members of the party and will not add greatly to individual loads, if pegs, tent, inner, and poles are divided among the members.

Materials and Condensation: Every lightweight camper has the occasional grouse about proofed nylon but very few of them would be willing to return to the days of cotton tents. Do we want a completely waterproof tent with the associated problem of condensation, or are we willing to forsake exterior waterproofness for a dry tent inside the flysheet, provided, of course, it doesn't rain?

The deciding factor is the weather in the areas where you normally camp. Will it always be dry and cold as in Northern Canada, or can you expect milder, wetter winter weather as in the U.K? My own preference is the all-nylon unit, for a pure cotton tent can be miserable. They are great when it is dry, but the cotton eventually lets in water, and then the inside always feels damp. On top of this, the weight of a cotton inner increases greatly when wet, and it takes a long time to dry out. Nylon tents, both inner and flysheet can be shaken almost dry, do not increase in weight when wet, and do not require the same time consuming care as cotton tents do. The condensation problem when you are inside can be reduced to a great extent by diligent airing. Providing an air flow is maintained between the two skins of the tent condensation will be minimal. Try sleeping with the doors of the tent open, or at least the flysheet door undone. Most of the warm air you exhale will then disappear into the night air. Cold air will circulate around the outside of the inner tent, as well as inside the tent itself. When you do this though, check that the wind-blown snow (spindrift) or rain is driving into the rear of the tent, and not through the open doors, or everything will get wet. Sleep head to exit, and you will notice driving rain or snow before all your gear is soaked.

In my experience of nylon tents, I can honestly say that only once have I suffered seriously from condensation. That was when I was testing a prototype model for a manufacturer and the inner tent was too large. As a result, the two skins of the tent were almost touching and the condensation from the inside of the flysheet was soaking through the inner where the two skins touched. So *good separation between the inner tent and fly is very important.* You may need to adjust the position of the inner after pitching to ensure this.

Cotton inners with nylon flysheets have a certain appeal, but I firmly believe that they are inferior to all-nylon units.

Gore-Tex material may well have a major effect on tent design and manufacture in the future. This breathable, waterproof material has been successful in the development of rainwear, but is, as yet, largely untried in winter tents. I have used *Gore-Tex* tents in summer conditions and have found them excellent, but I am still wary about their use in winter. Single skin tents in general don't appear to be for winter use, as the two skins of the normal tent must give added protection, and besides, if the flysheet rips apart in a gale there is always the inner, although, in theory, that would not last nearly as long as the flysheet. It would make life simpler to have a real super lightweight, single skin tent, strong enough to withstand the rigours of winter, but up to the present, the double skin tent is the best. For the future, anything is possible.

Entrances: There are two main types of winter tent entrance, the zipped door and the tunnel. Zipper entrances come in various sizes and shapes, ranging from the common inverted 'T' shape with three zips to the better inverted 'V' shape where two zips pull downwards from the apex. The advantage of the second type is that the zips can be pulled down only a short way, leaving an open space or 'window' for air flow. It also does away with the need for the 'ties' which should hold the door back in place but never seem to work effectively.

Tunnel entrances are useful for realy foul weather conditions, but are not very practical in nylon tents as the small opening makes air flow difficult to achieve.

Ordinary up-and-down zippers are quite adequate for the flysheet. Small hooks, fitted to either side of the bottom of the tent door flaps, are a good idea for holding the doors shut without putting excess strain on the zip.

Buying a Tent: Most of the better winter tents available in the stores today, are the result of many years experience, both in camping, and in manufacturing skills and design. A lot of work goes into the making of a good tent, and as a result, the cost is usually high. Bear this in mind when you buy a tent. The 'cheapies' are usually rather nasty, and even if they serve reasonably well in summer, they will probably start disintegrating at the first sniff of bad weather. So ask around, study the good magazines (see bibliography) and catalogues and make it your business to find out what is suitable before you buy.

When you have settled for a particular model, and you arrive at the store with your hard-earned cash clutched firmly in your fist, there are still some points to bear in mind before the sale takes place.

Examination in the Store: Although the real testing of a tent takes place in your own environment, a great deal of time and trouble can be saved by some careful examination in the store.

For real strength, and that is what we are looking for in a winter tent, major tent seams should be *lap-felled.* This means that the fabric edges should be folded around each other and then sewn together. The seams which hold the groundsheet to the tent wall should also be examined carefully as after a hard freeze-up at night, and in winter that means every night, the groundsheet sticks to the ground, making a hard jerk necessary to pull it free. A space blanket spread *under* the tent gives extra insulation and solves this problem.

The seams come under a lot of stress. In a well constructed tent, the stitching is evenly spaced, uniform in tension, and runs straight along the entire seam. Some tents have only four or five stitches to the inch on the seams, but the better ones have eight or nine. Check these seams and decide if the tent looks well made.

Crooked stitching, variations in tightness and puckered seams are potential weak points. Examine the seams carefully in the shop. Check thoroughly on the quality of the workmanship at the end of the zipper and in any corners. These areas are difficult to sew, and are sometimes sloppily finished. Very few manufacturers or retailers seal the seams in their tents for it is a costly and time consuming process, but all are willing to recommend a sealant. All winter tents should have their seams sealed, and this must be your first job after purchase.

Obviously it is best if you can examine a tent which is already pitched; then you can check that the fly fits snugly over the inner and pole assembly, that the fly pitches close to the ground and that the zips pull all the way down to the ground. Most important, estimate the tent's capabilities in snow and wind. It may sound difficult to test a tent for wind behaviour in the confines of a centrally heated camping store, but you can get a fair idea of how much the shape of the tent will be deformed in wind by pressing down on the *top* of the flysheet, and against the *side walls* between the poles. Tent walls which yield easily beneath the pressure of your hand will probably start flapping about once the wind starts blowing, and this constant buffeting will loosen the pegs and eventually collapse the tent.

Air Space: Check if there is enough space between the flysheet and the inner tent. When there is condensation on the inside of the fly, and the wind repeatedly blows it against the permeable inner tent, the wet will eventually 'wick' through the inner and start running down the inside wall. Before leaving the store make sure all the parts are there. Examine the pole sections and check that they fit together snugly. Even if you are fortunate enough to see the type of tent you want erected inside the store, remember it is unlikely that this will be the one you are sold. Your tent will probably be pulled from the shelf and handed over without inspection, so check it yourself *before* leaving the store.

Winter tents are not always easy to erect first time, especially on a mountain top in a Force 8 gale. This is not a good time to decipher pitching instructions, so buy your tent, take it home and practice pitching it until you can do it blindfolded, for — you never know — you may have to pitch it in the dark!

Extra Pegging and Guying Points: It's always handy to have a few extra pegging points sewn on to the bottom of the flysheet in case of really gusty weather. Rubber or neoprene rings attached to the pegging point (the ring which is sewn on the bottom of the flysheet) allow the tent to have some 'give' in gusty winds. If you peg the flysheet straight into the ground, only using the tap or 'd' ring which is normally fitted by the manufacturer, then a realy vicious wind could, due to lack of elasticity, either tear the peg out of the ground or rip the tent material. Most tents come complete with a guyline at the front of the tent, one at the back, and one on each side. This is usually enough for normal conditions, but in the event of a real wind it helps a lot if the guying points are the type which will allow you to put on some extra guylines.

Snow Valances: Snow valances also help in holding a tent to the ground. A *valance* is a wide skirt of material which extends on the ground from the bottom of the flysheet. Snow, or rocks can be piled on the valance to hold the sides of the tent taut. Be careful though, when using a snow valance. By sealing off the inside of the tent in this way, valuable air supplies may be severely curtailed if you fully zip up the door as well. If you must seal up the bottom of the tent by using the snow valanĉe, make certain that some air can come in the door. Whatever you do, don't light a petrol stove inside a tent which is completely sealed up with no fresh air circulating. In fact *never* light or refill a stove inside a tent. A sudden flare may set the whole tent ablaze.

SLEEPING BAGS

You can measure the warmth of a sleeping bag by its thickness or 'loft'. *Loft* refers to the bag's height *after* it has been fluffed up. Whatever the filling material, insulation is created by the innumerable tiny dead air pockets formed by the 'lofted' material which provides a barrier between body heat and the outside cold. Dry, still air is an excellent insulating medium and the more air pockets in the insulation the warmer you will be in the bag.

Construction: Baffles are sewn inside the bag to hold the insulation in place, and to make sure that the material is evenly distributed around the body. There are several methods of doing this and the bag's construction plays a significant part in providing warmth.

Sewn-through Construction: This method is the simplest, the cheapest and the least effective! The outside skin of the bag is sewn straight through to the inside skin which results in the sewn part having no insulation at all. This construction is no good for snow camping.

Laminated Construction: This consists of one sewn-through bag placed inside another with the seams offset. This method gives greater warmth, but the extra material involved makes the sleeping bag correspondingly heavier.

Box Construction: A box constructed bag has a vertical baffle which forms a wall between the inner and the outer shell, and so gives the bag a good uniform thickness throughout its length.

Slant Tube Construction: This employs a long slopng bag between the inner and the outer shell creating an overlapping tube effect. It allows the insulation to expand, is probably the best method of baffle construction, and results in a good winter bag.

Differential Cut: This simply means that the outer shell of the bag is cut with a larger diameter than the inner shell. This forms concentric shells of fabric allowing greater loft during use, while reducing the possibility of

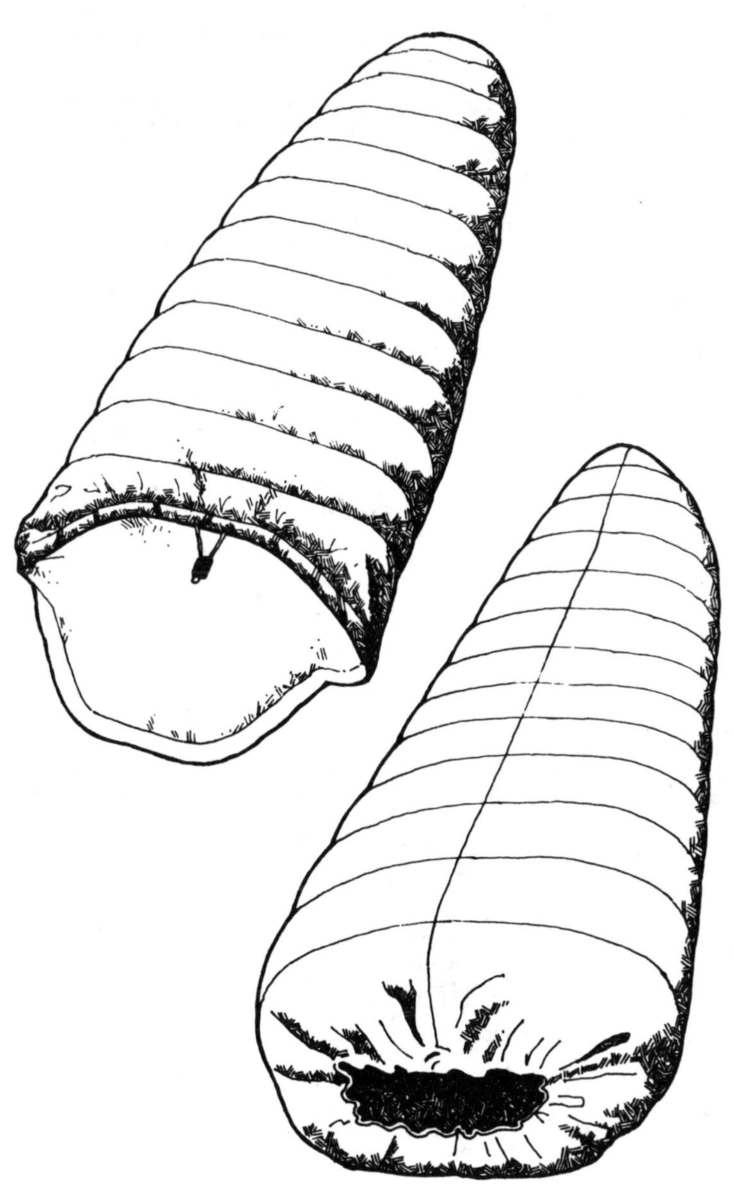

cold spots caused when a knee or elbow presses the inner fabric out against the outer shell. This method is good for winter use, always provided the filling is suitable.

Down Insulation: Down provides the best insulation for any given amount of weight. It allows moisture from the body to disperse, while creating air pockets which provide a barrier of still dry air between the body and the outside cold. Down is extremely light, very compressible for packing and very resilient, retaining 'loft' and insulating qualities for many years. There are various types of down, with variations in cost and performance. The finest filling material known at present is eider-down. Goose down is the finest filling currently used in sleeping bags, at least in terms of warmth/weight ratio and compressibility. It is only used in top grade sleeping bags, and is very expensive. Best quality goose down will contain an average of 95% of down overall, with not less than 85% at any one point. The rest will be made up of soft curled feathers.

Good duck down is not very far behind goose down in terms of filling qualities. As duck down is more common there is a wider range in quality.

Duck down and feather mixtures usually contain about 50% down, and the quality of the feathers varies tremendously. This is a cheaper filling, and gives a poorer insulation than pure goose or duck down. Feather and duck down mixtures are used in cheaper bags, the down content probably being less than 15%-20%.

So, for winter work, we must really think in terms of a bag filled with goose or duck down. The price of these materials has risen at a tremendous rate, and has now reached the stage where a top quality winter sleeping bag is a very, very expensive item.

Another disadvantage of down is its poor reaction to damp. When the soft down gets wet, it clumps together into a mass, and the insulation properties greatly decrease.

Synthetic Filling: Because of this, and the rising cost, outdoor people — especially in rainy temperate regions like the U.K., — started looking for a cheaper alternative, and synthetic fillings have proved to be just that, and very effective as well.

The best of these synthetics is *terylene,* the most widely used brands being *Dacron, Hollofil* and *Polarguard.* These fillings are not affected by damp.

Synthetic fillings do not absorb water as readily as down and because of the low absorbtion rate they retain loft even when saturated and will keep you warm even when wet through.

Their disadvantages are increased weight and bulk, and a decreased life span, but on the plus side, synthetic bags are much cheaper than down filled ones and they are also non-allergic.

Bag Features: The optional extras of a sleeping bag, are zips, hoods and the different types of foot.

I like having a zip on my sleeping bag. Unless you camp in extreme conditions all the time, the night will eventually arrive when the temperature is a bit higher than normal and you sweat inside the bag trying hard to keep cool. If you ever find yourself in this situation, you will wish you had a bag with a full length zip. However, beware of zips which are not backed by a 'draught tube'. The teeth of the zipper are obvious cold spots, so buy a bag with a generously fitted tube along the length of the zip. Nylon zips are obviously better than metal ones as they don't become so cold.

Hoods: Your winter sleeping bag should also have a hood or 'cowl' top which can be drawn around the head and securely tightened. Without it, valuable body heat will escape from the top of the bag, or from your head. You should be able to undo the closure quickly and efficiently in an emergency.

Foot Area: At the other end from the hood, most of the better bags have a special elliptical or square-shaped foot. This construction keeps the inner and the outer shells apart, and gives added warmth to the feet.

Shell Material: Most modern sleeping bags are covered in nylon. Weight for weight nylon is better than cotton cambric, the favourite material of yesteryear, but many manufacturers are now using a polyester cotton material for the *inside* of the bag. This makes the bag feel warmer on immediate entry, instead of the cold clammy feel of nylon. The nylon used for the shell of sleeping bags is not coated. There have been attempts in recent years to make a waterproof sleeping bag, but condensation usually damps the filling.

Bag Selection: A good sleeping bag is not the sole factor in keeping warm at night, and there are many other factors worth considering.

First, though, let us draw up some conclusions about sleeping bags, in the winter context. If you consider the weight/warmth ratio, and have plenty of money, then you will go for a good goose down or duck down bag. A bag with 2-2½lb (1 kilo) of down filling should be sufficient for winter use. If snow holing is likely to be your 'thing' then an expnsive down bag may not be such a good idea. You would be better with a polyester-filled bag which would withstand the damp conditions much better. A comparable polyester-filled bag would weigh about 4½-5lb (2 kilos) and would cost about half the price of the down one. In the end the choice of bag is wholly dependent upon the use you will put it to. A camp at sea level in a temperate climate is different in every sense from a winter camp in Alaska or the Arctic. Think about where and how you will use your bag and then choose wisely.

MATS OR PADS

Insulation: When your weary body is laid down to rest at night, the parts of the sleeping bag below your body will be compressed by your weight, so that in effect all that there is between you and the frozen ground or snow is some crushed feathers or terylene filling plus some very thin nylon. The secret of sleeping warm is insulation, especially insulation from the snowy ground. We need a mattress or sleeping pad. There are three basic types, *open-cell* and *closed-cell* foam mattresses, and air beds. Air beds can be a problem. Although they are reasonably thick, the air that is trapped inside is not still air. Your body warmth heats the air at the top of the mattress but the warm air comes into contact with the cold ground and it loses heat. Forget about airbeds for winter work.

The basic difference between open-cell foam mats and closed-cell foam is that the closed-cell foam has sealed cell chambers, while the open-cell type does not.

Open cells can soak up water, like a giant sponge. This is a great pity for the open cells make this type of foam bed very comfortable, although bulky.

Closed cell is the nearest we have to the best ground insulation available. Because the cells are sealed, water is not absorbed, so you have a good waterproof mattress. Also, as the air is trapped in the cells, you do not need a thick piece: ¼", ⅜", and ½" are the common sizes, and the thicker the better.

For size, bulk, and efficiency, closed foam wins hands down and although many campers like a full length piece for winter work, I find I can get by quite happily with a short, or hip-length piece. This cuts down the load that extra little bit, and more important, cuts down bulk. I put some spare clothing, waterproofs, parka, or whatever, below my legs and feet to provide insulation there.

METABOLISM

Some people sleep warm, others sleep cold, even in relatively warm conditions. If you are one of the unfortunates, what can you do about it? The human body has three methods of producing heat; from food, by movement, and by shivering. Sleeping bags are rather confining, so movement, to any great extent, is inhibited. Contracting and relaxing your muscles for a while certainly helps. Movement of this type performs much the same function as shivering. The difference is that shivering is uncontrollable and may well be a warning sign that exposure is around the corner. If you wake up during the night with the odd shiver this is normal, but if you have been in your bag for some time and *cannot* warm up, and then shivering begins, then beware. You may have a touch of hypothermia.

EATING

Let us consider the question of eating to keep warm. Food is vital to warmth. To maintain a stable body temperature, heat is dissipated through the skin. During the day, on the trail, this heat is produced by exercise, but in our sleeping bags the heat generating process is almost solely caused by the burning of fuel (or food). If you go to bed on an empty stomach, it is only natural that this heat generation will be curtailed, often resulting in a cold shivery wakening, long before dawn.

During the summer I usually walk well into the evening. Supper is normally taken after 9 p.m. with bed closely behind. This means I always get to bed with plenty of food inside me. In winter though, it is a different story. Early dark means an early pitch, so supper is usually about 5 to 6 p.m. Sleep comes about 9 p.m. This means a long time until breakfast and I wake up about 1 a.m. feeling peckish. Sweet tea and some chocolate fixes the hunger and gives the body something to work on until morning.

AIDS TO SLEEPING WARM

It is a fact of winter camping that beginners usually suffer more on cold nights than experienced campers. This has nothing to do with the gnarled old hiker being tougher or more warm blooded, but simply because experience teaches tricks and techniques which soon become automatic. It has little to do with equipment. Many old hikers use old, thin, sleeping bags, worn and frayed, and yet manage to sleep warm on the coldest of nights, while the beginner curls up in his super-bag and shivers the night away. Good gear certainly makes a very big difference, but you must know how to get the best from it.

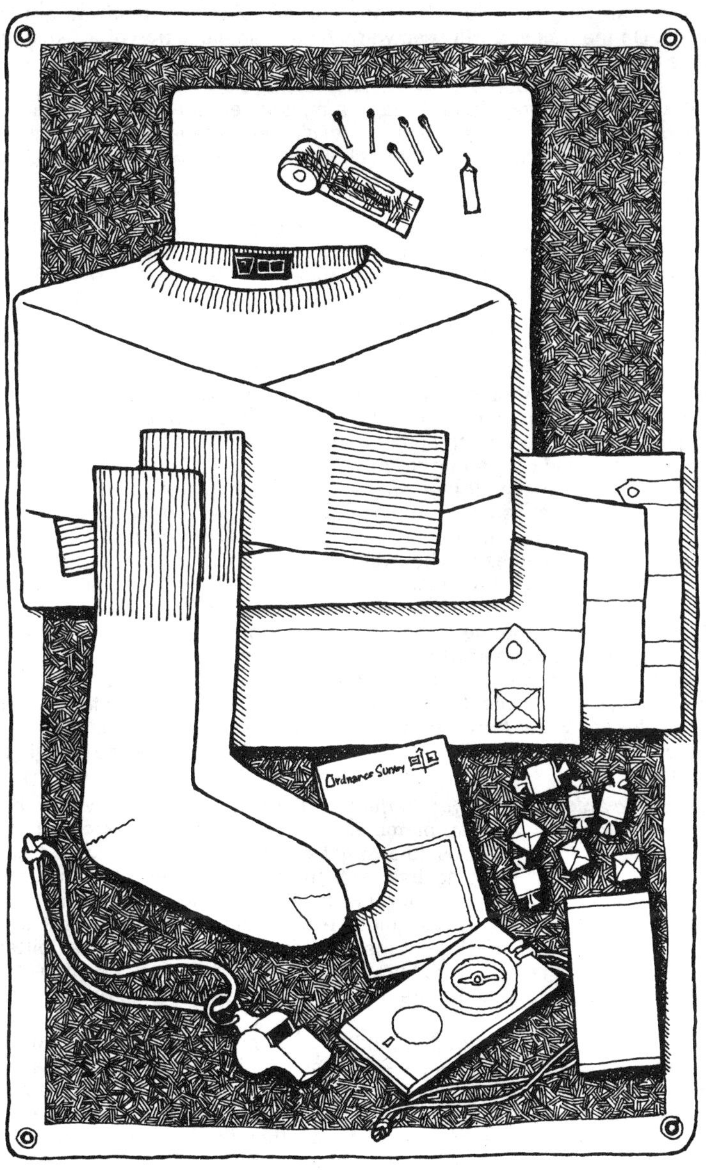
Ordnance Survey

The first thing to do is to get into your sleeping bag *while you are still warm.* On the trail you will keep warm by the simple action of walking, but once you stop to pitch camp, you will cool down rapidly in the cool of the evening and unless you change, your damp clothing will chill you very quickly. Keep moving, try and keep warm, and get into your bag as quickly as possible. A cold sleeping bag can take a long time to warm up if you are cold yourself, whereas if you are still warm, you will heat up the bag very quickly.

There is a fair bit of controversy as to whether you should wear damp clothing in your sleeping bag or not. Some say that you will dry off your clothes during the night and the moisture will evaporate and pass through the sleeping bag in the form of water vapour. Others take the view, to which I subscribe, that this moisture will eventually dampen the sleeping bag.

Valuable body heat is used up evaporating dampness from your clothing, which would be better used in keeping your body warm. The amount of drying out you can do in a sleeping bag is limited, and can only realistically be attempted when the clothes are very slightly damp, in which case they will dry quicker on your body in the morning. Sleep in a warm set of dry clothes and save the damp ones till morning.

If you feel cold coming up from below, check that you have not slipped off your insulation mat. If the mat is not thick enough to stop the cold from coming through, put some clothing below you as well. The next time, before you pitch your tent, line the surface of the ground with small evergreen boughs or pine needles or whatever else is handy, but make sure that they are small enough not to pierce the groundsheet of the tent. A space blanket, or your bivvy bag placed under the tent not only provides extra insulation, it will stop the tent freezing to the ground. This can lead to the proofing being damaged when you pull it free in the morning.

Some campers carry a hot water bottle with them. This is a good idea if you think you will be cold in your sleeping bag, but make sure that you get rid of the hot water bottle before it becomes cold. Once it is cold it will merely take away the heat from your body, but the water can be used in the morning.

Upgrading a Summer Bag for Winter Use: In those areas of the world where the temperatures do not plummet right through the bottom of the thermometer, it may be possible to get by using a three-season sleeping bag. Three-season sleeping bags, as the manufacturers call them, are supposed to be warm enough for use in spring, summer and autumn. This always seems to me to be a strange description, for in many areas spring may be just as cold as winter. Where I live, in Scotland, it is often bitterly cold and snowing even in late May, and my winter sleeping bag often stays in use right on into June before it gets bundled away for its brief summer hibernation.

A good 'three-season' bag should be a reasonably warm bag, and with some variations in technique, it should be possible to use this type of bag in the depths of winter in many areas, *but* if you intend heading for the more inhospitable regins of the world, like Alaska, Northern Canada, the Himalayas, or areas over say 2,000 metres, then the investment in a proper winter-weight sleeping bag is well worth making.

CLOTHING

Wearing warm clothing inside a sleeping bag is going to extend its range quite considerably. A fibre-pile suit should allow you to use a medium bag in reasonably cold conditions. A duvet, or down-filled suit will extend the range of the bag even more, but I would imagine most people would be better off buying a full weight winter bag than laying out the cost of a duvet suit.

Two sleeping bags, one inside the other, will make quite a difference, but make sure that one of the bags is smaller in size than the other. If you stuff one bag inside another of the same size, neither bag will loft sufficiently to give you the benefit of two bags. Sleeping bag liners, in fibre pile, are available in many stores, and these can make good summer-weight sleeping bags in their own right, *and* help a summer bag give winter warmth.

Finally, a sleeping bag *cover* will add extra insulation, but beware of so-called waterproof covers, or using bivvy bags. These bags have a specific purpose, usually of an emergency nature, and if you bunk down with your sleeping bag inside one of these you will end up with a wet bag, from condensation.

It is only common sense to use as much dry clothing as necessary to keep warm. If you feel cold, put on your spare clothing. There is not much point having dry clothing in your rucksack if you feel cold in your bag. Position sleeping bags close to each other to conserve warmth. Pile up your spare gear on the *tent wall* side of your sleeping bags, and have the bags together with nothing in the way. There's no place for modesty in a winter camp.

If you are still cold in your bag with all your clothes on, put on a hat. When the body gets cold, the arteries providing blood shift it to the body core, resulting in cold hands and feet. This means that the body is losing heat from somewhere faster than it is producing it. This heat loss, nine times out of ten, is through the head, so if your feet or hands feel cold, wear a hat.

One last point on sleeping warm. If someone is really cold, shivery, and just can't warm up, do not discount the possibility of hypothermia. A person whose 'inner core' temperature is dropping just cannot warm up in a sleeping bag, so someone will have to get in beside him. It is always *your* responsibility to look after your companion, and vice versa. A person suffering from exposure often becomes irrational and will not realise what is happening.

4 · Winter Living

Any camper who already has a fair amount of experience living out of doors, should not find any real difficulty in winter. Let us now look at some problems and solutions, and start with food.

Some problems will present themselves when cooking, like lack of water, but if there is plenty of snow on the ground, or ice on the ponds, a little bit of effort, a stove, (and plenty of fuel) will produce as much water as you need. In winter, careful planning and preparation at home will make life much easier in a winter camp. The weight element in food is contributed by the water content, so if we use as much dehydrated and freeze-dried food as possible, the lighter our packs are going to be, and in winter, with extra gear to carry anyway, you must save weight where you can.

A.F.D. FOOD (Accelerated Freeze-Dried Food)
A few years ago, the thought of living for even a weekend solely on freeze-dried and dehydrated foods would have been depressing, but such has been the advance in food technology for lightweight campers in recent years, especially from such firms as *Mountain House* and *Raven,* that this type of space-age food now makes up a considerable portion of my outdoor diet. All that is required to make A.F.D. food edible is a few pints of boiling water and one pot. You need the basic ingredients of course, and this is where the big disadvantage lies; cost! Dried foods are expensive, but that apart, A.F.D. food is ideal for snow camping.

PREPARATION
Ease of preparation is important in winter. The last thing you want is food which takes an eternity of simmering to cook it, for steam will float into or about the tent causing condensation. It is often possible to cook outside the tent but that's not *always* practical in winter. At the end of the day you will be feeling tired and the last thing you will want to do is squat outside in the cold, slaving over a cooker. Add to this falling snow, a mischievous wind and cold fingers, and it will be enough to put you off snow camping for life, so try the following routine.

Put some water on the stove as soon as you choose a pitch for the night. While you are pitching the tent, the water will be coming to the boil, allowing you to have a hot drink before you strip off your damp clothes and get into the bag. This drink is not only a great moral booster, but warms up the body so that it will heat up the sleeping bag that little bit sooner. The rest of the meal is then cooked inside the bell end of the tent from your sleeping bag.

BE CAREFUL WHEN LIGHTING THE STOVE — FIRE IS A KILLER!

Because the bell end of a lightweight tent is normally rather cramped, there is not too much room for extensive preparation like peeling potatoes, onions and so on. It is far better to do all the preparation in the warmth and comfort of your kitchen at home, then carry all the ingredients out in 'poly'

Batchelors
READY
DISHES
CHICKEN
SUPREME
PROTOVEG
CHUNKS
STYLE
Batchelors
SWEETS
CREME
CARAMEL
SAVOURY RISOTTO
Springlow
CURRIED
RICE AND
BEEF
Springlow
SPACE AGE FOODS
FREEZE DRIED
LIVER with ONION GRAVY
Cup-a-Soup
THICKER
&
TASTIER
Atkinsons
RAISIN & RUM
FLAVOUR FUDGE

bags. All you have to do in camp is put them in a pot and cook, and with A.F.D. food, you only need hot water.

The ideal meal when snow camping is the one-pot stew, a cross between a soup and a casserole. This thick soup-like stew provides extra liquid in the diet which is an important factor in winter. Dehydration is a constant enemy and plenty of salt in the stew will replace much of what is lost during the day through perspiration.

A cold food diet is not to be encouraged for winter camps. I read of a camper who swore he could get by all year on a diet of fresh fruit and vegetables. He scorned the idea of a stove, calculating that the weight saved could be used in carrying extra food, but eventually he had to eat his words as he had nothing else to eat, his fruit and veg. having frozen solid during the night and he didn't have a stove to thaw them out!

FOOD PLANNING

It is always a good idea to get together with your mate a few days before you head out and plan a menu, choosing one which suits both of you. Nutritional requirements are not so important on weekend trips, as the body can get by for a short while on all sorts of diet, but for more extended trips a high calorific content is important, together with a good smattering of essential vitamins. It helps matters greatly if you have an idea of the use the body makes of the various food categories; fats, proteins and carbohydrates, and of the calorific value of the food you eventually take. Food = calories = energy. You will need around 4000-5000 calories a day for energy and warmth while winter camping.

Carbohydrates (sugar and starches) are the easiest foods to digest, followed by *proteins.* These will give you a quick energy boost. *Fats* take a considerable time to digest properly, but on the other hand fats contain twice the calorific content of either protein or carbohydrates. Carbohydrates are the best foods for instant energy, and for instant fuel while the body is working hard. This is why goodies like chocolate, glucose sweets, and biscuits make good trail nibbles. They are all high in carbohydrates, and give you a quick energy boost if you are flagging on the trail.

Proteins are used to rebuild the tissues in the body. Extra warmth is produced by the digestion of protein, so it is a good idea to eat something rich in protein before settling down at night to prevent nocturnal chills. High protein foods like bacon, salami, cheese, powdered milk and eggs stave off hunger for long periods of time.

Fats produce over twice as many calories as carbohydrates or proteins. They also take longer to digest and provide a fair amount of warmth during the digestion. Good fatty foods include nuts, oil, butter, peanut butter, and I find fatty foods quite enjoyable when I am out for a winter jaunt. Because of their long digestion times, fatty foods provide an amount of energy later in the day, so eat fat and high protein foods for breakfast with carbohydrates eaten at regular intervals throughout the day to stop your 'energy bank' becoming overdrawn.

CALORIES

The dieticians tell us that a man of average weight with a sedentary job such as an office clerk, will require about 2,000 calories a day to operate effectively. Someone who wanders slowly along a track in summer may use up to 3,500 calories, but a winter camper or mountain backpacker will require up to 5,000 calories per day. Now, 5,000 calories require a fair bit of eating, but it is impossible to live healthily on the trail in winter if you are skimping on food. Let us take a look at the calorific content of some camping foods:

Carbohydrates	*Calories per 1oz/30grms*
Cocoa	128
Dates	89
Honey	80
Jam	80
Milk Chocolate	150
Muesli	160
Pasta	100
Instant Potatoes	95
Fresh — boiled potatoes	25
Crisps	160
Raisins	84
Rice grains	98
Brown Sugar	110
Fats	
Butter	225
Cooking oil	250
Cashew Nuts	170
Egg (dried)	166
Peanuts	168
Peanut Butter	173
Protein	
Fresh bacon	80
Cheddar cheese	115
Blue cheese	105
Cream cheese	230
Corned Beef	75
Beef Stew	80

The above list will give an approximate idea of the calorific value of normal food. Using such a list it is possible to work out a menu which will match requirements in the winter backcountry and provide adequate energy and warmth.

For a winter trip the diet should ideally consist of the following:-

Carbohydrates — about 60% of the total food intake, or about 1lb (500 grms) per man per day.

Fats — about 20% of food intake or about ¼lb (120 grms) per man per day.

Protein — about 40% of food intake, or just over ½lb (240 grms) per man per day.

Total food *weight* should be arund 1.75 lbs. per person per day. Note that 2.2 lb = 1 kilo.

This kind of diet is ideally suited to the winter camper but it does not mean that the body will break down if these proportions are not rigidly followed. The body can take wide variations from this breakdown, and still function well.

The important thing is to enjoy your food. It's good to look forward to a meal at the tail end of the day, and lots of tea with chocolate biscuits after the main meal make the long evenings enjoyable.

WATER

Cold winter air is dry. In addition you will be perspiring all day, so that the body uses up a considerable amount of liquid. Winter walkers pass very little water but the loss through dehydration and perspiration must be replaced. Drink plenty of fluids during the day and with meals.

One of the advantages in camping under snow conditions in temperate zones is that water is rarely a problem. In the winter though, most water sources can freeze, or be under snow or thick ice. If water is readily available, it should certainly be used in preference to melt-water from snow, since melting snow takes time, effort, and a lot of fuel.

The novice snow camper will take a full pot of snow, stick it on the stove, and wonder why he has run out of fuel with very little water to show for his efforts. What happens is that the snow will act like a blotter, soaking up the water at the bottom of the pan as it melts. It is far better to melt crushed ice, crushing it first with crampons or your ice axe. When using snow, the trick is to start with only a small amount, barely enough to cover the bottom of the pan. As this melts, add more, a small amount at a time, until you have enough water for your brew. Wet snow, the soggy stuff which falls when the temperature is around freezing point, is best and you should use any heat source available to melt ice or snow and keep your water containers full.

The next best thing to use is crusty snow. Dry powder snow is fairly useless since you need to melt a surprising amount of it for even a little water. Ice is not difficult to melt, but it will melt quicker if there is a little hot water already in the pot. Try chipping bits of the ice into a pan a little at a time. Once there is an inch or so of warm water in the bottom of the pan you can make the ice chips larger.

The common mistake that people make when using melted snow or ice for drinking water is melting too little at a time. Keep the stove going, keep adding the snow or ice and, as it boils, take enough for your hot drink remembering to leave a fair amount in the bottom of the pan. Instead of turning the stove off until you begin your next course, keep it going, continually adding more snow. You can never get enough water in a winter camp. You need roughly up to a gallon per person per day, especially when exercising hard and sweating a lot.

ALCOHOL

It has been said by all the authorities that one should not consume alcohol in the mountains! The same goes for tobacco. Smoking apparently constricts the capillaries in the skin's surface and reduces blood flow to the extremeties, while alcohol increases heat loss by dilating the capillaries. Now you know! And now that I have done my duty by quoting the 'official' view, let me add that a small glass of whisky and a smoke from a pipe or cigar adds a luxurious dimension to my post-supper relaxation in the tent. That glass and smoke, to me anyway, is a great morale booster and I'm not going to do without it.

STOVES

I assume that you do not intend cooking on an open fire! Apart from the ecological reasons, fires are difficult to light in winter, totally useless in emergency situations, blacken pots and sometimes food beyond recognition, and take a great deal of skill to operate. A light well-designed backpacker's stove is a much better bet all round.

What you should look for in a good design is light weight, stability, ease of operation, and good heat output in sub-zero conditions. This last consideration almost puts butane gas out of the running. While clean, easy to operate and efficient in summer conditions, it just doesn't have sufficient pressure when the temperature plummets, making water boiling a long frustrating experience. With a great deal of love and tender care, butane gas canisters can be kept warm in the sleeping bag until it is time for it to be used, but usually after five or ten minutes they cool down again, with a diminishing flame and heating power.

Methylated spirit stoves, such as the ever popular *Trangia* and *Turmsport* models, enjoy an amazing amount of popularity among winter campers being both efficient and functional. They also have the great advantage of not requiring a separate windshield, for a windshield is, in fact, part of the stove. The pots sit cosily inside, where the heat of the burner literally wraps around the bottom of the container, giving the maximum heat to the surface available. The main problem with these stoves is bulk, and the fact that the *Trangia* is thirsty. Although the pots are integral, the cost and weight of methylated spirits and the large appetite that the stove has for fuel tends to make a large supply of fuel necessary. For winter campers who need to be weaned away from their summer butane, I would strongly recommend the *Trangia* Meths stove, as it is safe, easy to operate and very stable, with not parts to lose or go astray.

Petrol stoves tend to be volatile creatures, but apart form this aspect, they are sound, functional burners. Petrol gives off toxic fumes when it is burning, so you will require plenty of ventilation when cooking. Modern petrol stoves are normally self-priming, which means that the pressure driving the fuel from the tank to the burner is provided by the stove's own heat. This is fine once the stove is lit, but lighting the the stove can be a problem. Pre-warm the fuel pipes with Meta tablets first until the vapour flows out of the jet. The *Svea 123* is a very popular make, and will work well once warmed in this way.

Petrol stoves burn well in most temperatures, but tend to heat up quickly and then melt downwards into the snow, but a small square of closed cell foam underneath should solve this problem. Anodised aluminium bottles, like the *Sigg* bottles, clearly marked, are best for carrying petrol. They should be marked *Petrol, Kerosene,* or whatever.

Paraffin (kerosene) stoves, burn almost as well as petrol stoves, but have some seasonal disadvantages. Paraffin is slower to evaporate and therefore slower to ignite than petrol. Many petrol stoves are self pre-heating and work quickly once warmed. Paraffin stoves need an additional pre-heating fuel, solid fuel tablets or meths. Paraffin is also a bit messy; it feels greasy, it smells, and if you spill a drop or the fuel bottle leaks a little inside your pack, then everything else will be contaminated, including the food. On top of this, paraffin burns with a sooty flame and really blackens pots.

With these disadvantages, it is perhaps surprising that anyone uses paraffin at all, but there are advantages. Paraffin is the least dangerous of

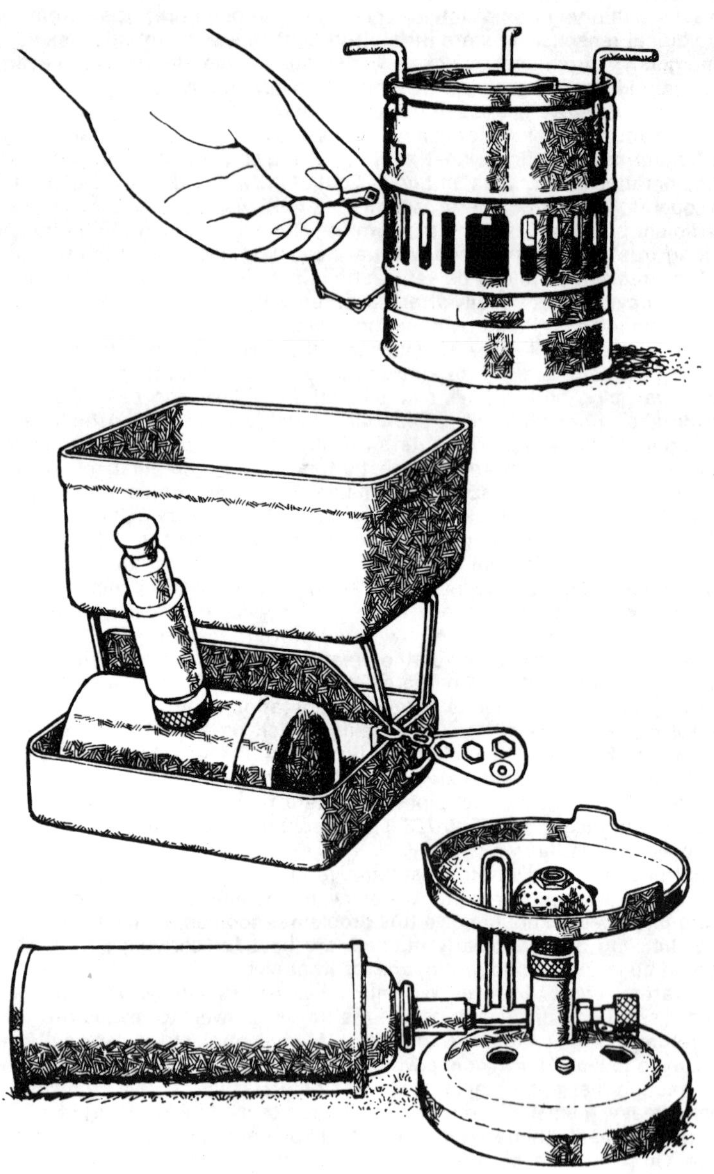

all fuels, with the exception of meths. When lit, paraffin burns brightly and well, and although the heat output is virtually the same, it is not nearly as volatile as petrol. You could spill some and it wouldn't flare up, and there is little chance of your stove overheating to a dangerous level. You can also use paraffin in your lamps, thus avoiding the need for two fuels, and with a saving in weight.

If you are heading out with a group, especially a group which includes no ices, then paraffin may be a good fuel to use, because of the safety and double use angle.

Finally, a word of warning. When the weather is very cold, don't let any petrol spill on your bare skin. Petrol left outside overnight could be well below zero come morning, and if this is spilled on bare flesh it will cause additional cooling by evaporation. Frostbite is then quite likely, severe burning almost certain. Take a funnel to fill the stove, and never fill or light the stove in the tent.

POTS AND UTENSILS

The *Trangia* stove comes complete with its own pots, but for other stoves you will require a cook set consisting of at least one pint pot, one lid-cum-frying pan, a plastic mug, and a dessert type spoon. Forks, dinner knives etc., are a matter of choice and your summer kit will do very well, although plastic is better than chilly metal.

COOKING INSIDE

The most popular position for camp cooking, especially in the depths of winter, is in a prone position in the sleeping bag. This requires a bit of practice and a certain amount of skill, especially if you happen to be sharing a tent. I have found that it is best to nominate one person in turn to do the cooking, while the others lie in their sleeping bags and read, snooze, or generally keep out of the way. Cooking in a small tent is a one man job and should not be attempted until the inside of the tent is well organised.

The obvious fire risk from a stove must be respected and whenever possible, keep the stove in the bell end of the tent, for a tent fire is unthinkable. Melting nylon is horrible, and melting nylon on your skin is very, very painful, so please be careful.

STOVE ACCESSORIES

If your stove is of the self-pressuring type, then an interesting little piece of kit from *Optimus* may help make life a bit easier in the wilds of winter. This is a special Mini Pump, which helps to start self-pressure stoves in cold weather. When conditions are really cold, it can take a bit of time to start up the self-pressure type, but this mini-pump means that you can physically build up the pressure in the stove in a matter of seconds. It doesn't make the stove burn any hotter, but can turn a good summer stove into an efficient winter one. Unfortunately it only fits the *Optimus* or *Svea* range of stoves.

We have already mentioned fuel bottles, but many people go off and forget to carry a funnel for filling the stove. It is dangerous to pour petrol or paraffin from the bottle into the fuel tank without a funnel, as no matter how careful you are, some fuel always seems to spill. This is wasteful and potentially dangerous. A small metal or plastic funnel doesn't cost very much, weighs virtually nil, and will make life much easier.

AMOUNT OF FUEL

Fuel is always a problem for winter campers. They either carry enough to fuel an army for a month, or they spend the last couple of days of their trip carefully minimising the amount of cooking in an effort to use as little fuel as possible. How much fuel you will need depends on various factors; whether you enjoy long camping banquets using fresh food, or whether you simply cook for the minimum of time using freeze dried or dehydrated food, though for this you need plenty of hot water. I know I certainly enjoy spinning out the long winter evenings by cooking big meals, and therefore, have to carry more fuel. Altitude is another factor which you must consider. Cooking times increase as pressure drops, so the higher you go the longer it takes to boil water, so the more fuel you will use. You must also remember that melting snow or ice for water uses up a lot of fuel.

Generally speaking, *a cupful of fuel per person per day* is enough, with some spare for any emergency which may arise.

WINDSHIELD

Draughts and winds blowing around the tent make the use of a windshield virtually essential. Even when cooking in the bell end of the tent, there is almost always a slight draught blowing down between the two skins of the tent. Quite often a well placed boot is enough to deter a minor draught from affecting the flame, but proper windshields are light and functional, and they don't take up much space in the pack. Many, of course are available commercially, but a large wad of aluminium foil, held upright by some spare tent pegs, can do an admirable job. Even better is the type supplied with some stoves in the form of a three part, hinged, aluminium square. This sits snugly around the stove and allows easy access for cooking. Anything which stops the draught affecting the flame will work, as long as the material of the windshield is flame retardent or non-inflammable. *A WORD OF WARNING:* Whenever you improvise a windshield, make absolutely certain that there is sufficient ventilation around the fuel tank. The tanks on self-pressure stoves need to be warm to work, but should never be allowed to become too hot to touch. *Trangia* or *Optimus* meths cookers have built in windshields.

LIGHTING

In my opinion, there is nothing to beat the humble candle for tent illumination and warmth. Even the flickering glow from a candle has enough light and if you place it in a pot or cup in the porch of the tent, it will not cause any harm.

My own recent tests show that a squat four by two and a half inch *stearine* candle will burn in still conditions for up to twenty hours, but you should knock off a couple of hours for the draughty conditions likely to be found in a tent. Along with the candle, I carry a small square of aluminium foil which, placed *behind* the flame, will reflect a fair amount of heat and light into the tent, certainly enough for comfortable reading. The main disadvantage of a candle is the fact that there is an open flame, and where there is naked flame there is danger. Candle light tends to flicker where there is a draught and this can be overcome to a great extent by sheltering the candle with the aluminium foil from your stove windshield.

GAS LANTERNS

If an open flame does not appeal to you, then consider a butane gas lantern or a paraffin lamp. There will always be a place in my pack for a functional lightweight gas lamp, but alas, to date I haven't found one. The ones I have tried have been disappointing, as I always manage to break the fragile mantles.

FLASHLIGHTS

Torches and flashlights are probably the most reliable means of tent illumination, and also the most expensive. Having said this, a torch is an indispensible piece of winter gear and something which should be carried by every outdoor person, even on day trips, as emergency equipment. In summer I use a small pocket-size flashlight, which lives beside my pillow, inside my boot, at hand for any emergency which may occur. In winter a much more substantial light is required. My torch's duties during the long cold nights can range from illuminating the site while I erect the tent in the dark, to checking for leaks or condensation in the early hours of the morning. There are a number of large battery-powered lamps available, but most of these are too heavy. What is required, is something which will give a good beam, last for a reasonably long time and at the same time be light and compact. I have found the answer in the shape of a head torch. The bulb and lense is fitted to an elasticated strap which goes round the head, and a long wire connects it to a simple four and a half volt battery. This combination gives a good steady beam for up to eight hours. Cold temperatures have an adverse effect on the life of a battery, reducing it considerably unless it can be warmed. My torch battery is a constant bedmate in winter, as only the warmth from my body can keep it fully effective.

5 · Winter Equipment

As the previous chapters have indicated, much of the camper's 'three-season' gear will be just as suitable in winter. Some items — sleeping bags for example, can be reinforced or adapted, and certain items like gas stoves, are better changed for more suitable fuels. There remains equipment which, if optional at other times, will form the basic tools of the snow camper, and they are:-

1. The ice axe.
2. Crampons.
3. Snow shovel.

The first two are vital pieces of kit, the third a very useful addition, but for any of them to be effective they must not only be carried at all times, but used, and used properly. Skills with axe, crampons and shovel need to be learned and practised, for in the snow and ice covered hills of winter they give you your only real security.

Many campers or backpackers get tremendous enjoyment from their sport without even venturing near a hill or mountain, and why not? Others climb hills only in summer, leaving the snowy slopes of winter to the 'extreme backpacker' or mountaineer. A steep icy snow slope can and should be a daunting prospect initially, but once the basic skills of ice axe braking and cramponing are learned, then, (and only then) will the whole range of winter travel become possible. It is a great pity to avoid the challenge of the mountains under snow because of a natural wariness of steep slopes, but that natural fear of a slip can be overcome once you have gained confidence in ice axe handling and crampon techniques.

SNOW SLOPES

A line must be drawn between the slope which can be easily negotiated by the walker with ice axe and crampons, and a slope which will require mountaineering skills, the use of rope, ice hammers and 'front pointing' on crampons. Snow which may seem steep to a walker will not necessarily seem steep to the experienced ice climber. Ice climbing techniques are outside the scope of this book, so let us stick with snow slopes which can be walked upon in an upright position, without having to use the hands for support. If your slope is steeper than this you are in the wrong place! This type of slope may be covered with soft snow which allows step kicking or hard snow which requires step cutting or cramponing. Hard snow at even an easy angle may still be dangerous int he event of a slip, because of the drop or rocks below. The winter walker needs to consider the 'if' factor and 'if' you slip, what happens?

THE "IF" FACTOR

What will happen if you slip is something to consider all the time, so make sure you can recognise inherently dangerous slopes. An ice axe is not much help when you come rolling down the hill in company with thousands

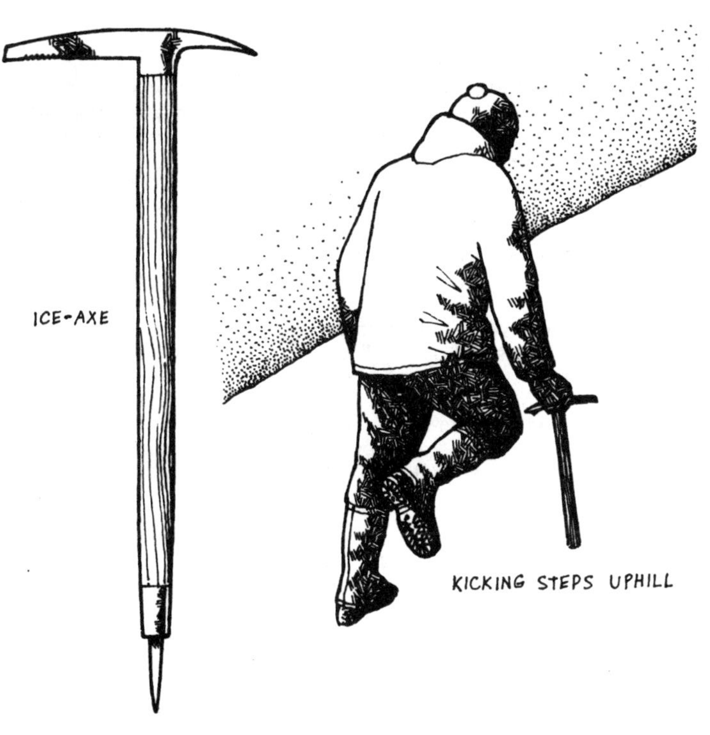
ICE-AXE
KICKING STEPS UPHILL

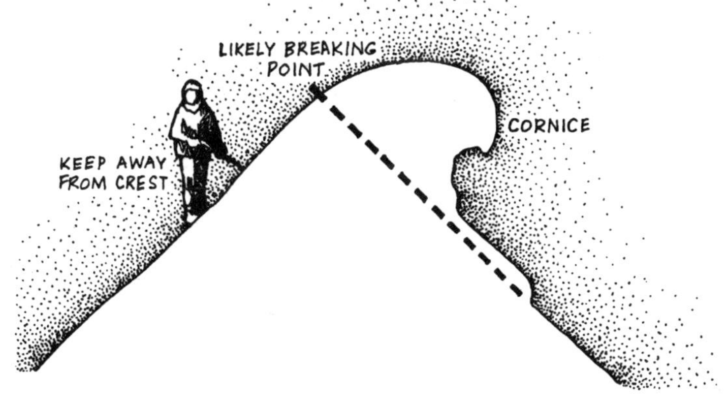
LIKELY BREAKING POINT
CORNICE
KEEP AWAY FROM CREST

of tons of snow, or if you slide, braking hard, into an unyielding rock. Wearing a cagoule you exert no friction on hard snow and are virtually in free fall, with only the axe to hold you.

THE ICE AXE

An ice axe has a shaft of wood or metal with a "pick and an adze" head at one end, and a spike at the other. As far as winter walkers are concerned, it is a safety tool used for *braking* in the event of a slip on steep snow, and as an implement for *cutting steps* on hard snow or ice.

There are many types of axe available today, but generally the walker's axe is a bit longer than the climber's. Climbers use their axes to cut holes in confined spaces like gullies, so a shorter axe is more useful to them, while the walker's axe is almost a walking stick. The correct axe length for the walker is one which will just clear the ground when held straight down by your side.

The head of the axe has an adze and a pick. The pick should be serrated to improve grip on the snow or ice. The handle of the axe may be wood, metal, or even fibre-glass. Wood tends to be warmest. Whatever it is, wrap some adhesive tape around part of it to improve your grip. A slipping axe haft can be an added problem when braking.

Although many experienced climbers do not attach the ice axe to their wrist in any way, the walker would be well advised to use a wrist loop, so that in the even of dropping the axe, you will not lose it.

USING THE AXE

Temporary carrying positions *off the slopes* include under one arm, lashed to the rucksack by the ice axe straps, or tucked between the rucksack and the back. Once on a snow slope the axe must be carried in the hand. For walking across slopes, or up slopes, the axe is held carried across the body, axe-head at shoulder height, one hand on the axe-head with the pick downwards, the other low on the shaft. In the event of a slip this gives an instant braking position, and the axe can be swiftly employed to halt your slide.

When climbing soft snow slopes the axe can be driven into the snow and used to pull up on. Going down it can be used as a steadying hold. While traversing, and most steep slopes have to be traversed, you are better to hold the axe across the body with the *spike* pressing into the slope, but on steep slopes, where a slip could mean a long slide, reverse this and keep the *pick* to the slope in an immediate braking position.

KICKING STEPS

On soft snow, plant the axe, and kick into the snow. Kick in hard, lodging your foot well and keeping the heel high, so that your foot cannot slip back out of the hole. Test your weight on this foot just in case the snow will not take your weight, and then move up a step, kicking in to the snow again to be once more secure on both feet. When you have stepped up and are properly balanced, not before, move your axe and plunge it in to the snow above you again. Never move your axe and your feet at the same time. Always have *two* points of contact in the snow at all times.

Coming down soft snow, make sure you are always in a balanced position and don't lean back too far. Dig the heels well into the snow, and carry the axe in a braking position. Walking on snow takes practice but with practice you will soon gain confidence and start to move well.

CUTTING STEPS

As the snow becomes harder, and it is impossible to kick steps, then crampons must be worn and steps must be cut in the snow with the ice axe. Move diagonally across the slope and take great care as to the spacing and size of the steps; remember you may have to descend on them again or your companions may use them after you. Use one hand to cut the step and let the balance and weight of the axe do the work. Hard aggressive actions are not necessary unless the snow is very hard indeed and two or three blows should be enough to cut out a fair sized step, each glancing blow carving out a platform without fracturing or weakening the surrounding crust. Here again, test the step before you trust your weight to it and keep two points of contact at all times.

BRAKING

You can slip from any position and end up sliding on your front, your back, or head first, but the basics of braking remain the same. In the event of a slip roll face in to the snow across the axe and apply *gradual pressure* to the axe head, keep the arms low and use body weight on the axe. If you apply sudden pressure it will cause the axe pick to bury in the snow suddenly and it could well be snatched from your grasp or, on hard ice, fail to grip at all. Whatever position you fall in, head up or down the slope, on your front or back, roll so that your head is uphill and you can use a conventional self-arrest brake. It is possible to use the axe to turn into the head-up-slope position. If you are falling with your head downslope, reach out and *gradually* dig the pick into the snow, in front, and slightly to one side. This action will begin to slow you down, and force your body round into the correct position for self-arrest. As you can imagine, this is far from easy and the situation is quite hazardous. There is no easy way to learn self-arrest. It takes lots and lots of practice. The actual event itself is far from pleasant and you will be glad of that practice when it occurs.

PRACTICE

It is absolutely essential to continually practise braking techniques. Fine a concave slope with a clear, soft run out at the bottom. Cover any small protruding rocks with your pack or clothing and practise, practise, practise. Fall down on your back, your front, your side, somersault, slip with a pack, without a pack, until you can stop yourself in any situation. Practise on soft snow and hard snow. Ice axe braking is the most basic, and the most important lesson on snow walking, so make sure you can do it. Practise, for one day you may need to do it to save yourself from injury.

One point to remember is that if you fall wearing crampons, keep your feet clear of the gound or else they will dig into the slope as you slide and you will go head over heels. Practise this as well!

CRAMPONS

Crampons are spiked soles, which fit on the bottom of the boot with straps. They come with either ten or twelve points. On twelve-point crampons the front pair stick out forward like lobster claws and are used for the ice climbing technique known as 'front pointing'. Ten-point crampons are the ones for the winter walker. They should have quick release bindings and be adjustable so that they can be changed from one pair of boots to another. To put on a crampon, lay it on a flat surface and open out all the straps. Check that when the straps are fastened the buckles will be on the outside

BRAKING WITH THE ICE-AXE

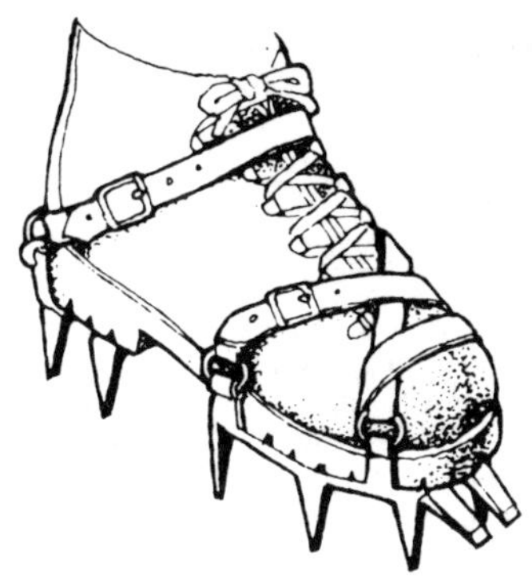

CRAMPONS

of the boot, otherwise you could trip over them quite easily. Place your foot in the crampon and pull up the heel wire to the top of the heel piece on your boot. The strap loops should fit close to the boot. Fasten the heel strap, then the cross over straps, passing this last under the bottom of the boot lacing, which will stop the strap coming off at the toe. Stamp and shake the boots around and make sure that the crampons are firmly attached.

Crampons must be used by walkers on icy ground where vibram soles will slip around like skates. Walking on icy slopes traverse rather than go straight up, walking in a zig-zag fashion, with the ice axe always at the ready.

In soft snow crampons "ball-up" with snow and should not be worn, but if this happens on firm slopes, rap the crampons with the ice axe to clear the points. Do not let snow clog the spikes. You should also wear gaiters and tuck any laces away. If a spike catches a trouser flap or a loose lace it could cause you to fall.

Practise walking in crampons up, down and across slopes. Flex your ankles to accommodate the angle of the snow and walk with a slight stamping action so that all the crampon points bite simultaneously. With crampons as with ice axes, practice is the secret of success. Never go into the hills in winter without your ice axe and crampons and be sure you know how to use them.

SNOW SHOVELS

For obvious reasons the snow shovel is a piece of equipment which comes into its own in winter. It is possible to dig shelters, excavate caves and build windbreaks without a shovel, but only at the expense of getting wet either from melting snow or perspiration! There is now a wide variety of light, strong and collapsable snow shovels on the market, and one should certainly be carried in winter, as a group item. In the event of trouble it is a real boon, enabling the party to dig out a shelter or protect themselves very quickly, and with the minimum expenditure of energy.

6 · Camp-Craft

Winter is the season of the short days and the long, long nights. This is all very well if you like lots of sleep, but the early dusk means that you cannot afford to spend as much time looking for and selecting a pitch as you can during the summer months. Come mid-afternoon, at the latest, be prepared to call it a day. It is always better to enjoy the last moments of daylight from the warmth and comfort of a tent, than keep walking until the last shreds of daylight have gone for pitching in the dark can be difficult, to say the least. Add a mischievous wind, falling snow and soggy underfoot conditions, and you may well have the beginnings of an epic. This happened to me on a trip not so long ago. I had had a long hard day and planned on staying at a pitch I knew well. Darkness beat me to it and I ended up pitching on the first flat piece of ground I came across. I stamped the snow flat and when it was firm and hard, pitched my tent with the aid of my head torch and had a reasonably comfortable night. Come morning however, things didn't look so good. A thaw had melted the snow and revealed that I had pitched on a marsh! The rear tent pole had sunk for a quarter of its length into the ooze and the rear guyline with two of the side guys had pulled out. The flysheet had therefore collapsed against the inner tent, soaking it with condensation, and my skis, which had been stuck in the snow the previous night, sloped drunkenly to one side. It was a pathetic, miserable scene, but changeable weather is a feature of the winter scene.

I was very lucky that the night was not too windy, or the whole lot might have taken off into the night with me inside, but had I pitched in daylight I would have noticed the open bog less than twenty metres away. I re-learned that lesson — to pitch early — without any real discomfort, but you might not be so lucky. Find a good pitch and stick with it, even if it is as early as mid-day when you come across it. You may not find another before dark.

SELECTING A PITCH

The main consideration in winter is the availability of water. Melting snow or ice for drinking water can be a long and tedious process which uses up a great deal of precious fuel. The second consideration is to check that there are no dangers or avoidable unpleasantness about. By this I mean that you should not pitch on an avalanche slope, under snow falling from trees, when exposed to excessive wind, or in areas which will attract drifting snow.

We will discuss avalanches in another chapter, but remember to stay well clear of any pitch at the direct foot of a slope, out of narrow gullies, or on steep treeless slopes which make natural avalanche paths. All the snow which falls on mountain slopes will either melt, or sooner or later come sliding down to settle in a more stable position. Make certain that your little tent is not down there when it happens.

Avoid camping under trees. Many people are mistaken in thinking that a few trees are just the thing for a bit of shelter but they forget that snow, especially soft wet heavy snow, often falls from the tree tops, and if your tent is directly underneath, the possibilities are that it will be flattened. Stay in the lee of trees, but not directly underneath, and beyond the drift line such lees create. The other danger from trees is that a strong wind may well tear off branches, or even worse, blow an old tree down.

Driving snow can bury a tent within minutes, and to stop it collapsing you or your mate must leave the warmth and comfort inside at regular intervals to clear the snow away. Your snow shovel is handy here. It is best not to get into this situation in the first place, although sometimes, especially in really stormy weather, it is unavoidable, but remember that snow drifts tend to build up on the lee side of objects. A little wind keeps the snow moving. You may think you have a nice sheltered spot, but make sure it will not attract drifts or allow snow to settle unless you enjoy getting up in the middle of the night to move house. A drifted-in tent can be potentially dangerous for the snow ices up on the fly, the tent becomes airtight, and suffocation becomes a very real threat, especially if you have naked lights inside. Take the shovel *into* the tent in case you have to dig yourself out again.

With a bit of searching you may be able to find a pitch free from such risks, with running water close at hand. If there is no wind about, cutting down on the chance of drifting snow, bear in mind also that cold air sinks. The little sheltered bowl which looks ideal may, in fact be ten degrees cooler than the apparently exposed ledge 30ft higher, and any little gully which runs into the bowl may well become a river for cold air flowing down during the night. Therefore try not to pitch on the valley bottom, but a few feet higher, away from the gulley or stream which provides your water, just beyond a lee and off risky slopes.

PITCHING ON SNOW

Once you have selected your pitch, someone should set about the routine task of fetching water and putting on the brew. While your friend is fetching the water, flatten out the snow on your pitch using the soles of your boots, or even better, the flats of your skis, or better still, both. This platform should be slightly larger than the tent itself, and the more you stamp on it the more compact and firm the platform becomes. Make sure it is even and flat, for the surface will soon freeze, and lumps and bumps will feel like concrete under your body when you settle in for the night.

After walking all day, your feet will become cold very quickly once you stop. By the time the tent is up, your feet will probably be freezing, hands and fingers numb, and the condensation chilling inside your clothing. A warm brew at precisely that moment makes all the difference between a miserable experience and a happy one, but get the outside work done first.

PEGGING OUT

Have a set routine for establishing your pitch, so (after putting on a brew and preparing the ground) you will next erect your tent. Stop the tent bags from blowing away by putting them underneath your packs. Assemble the poles, and leave them in roughly the position they will be erected. Roll out the fly sheet, kneeling on it if it is windy. Peg out the corners, windward side first. There are several methods of staking out a tent, depending on the weather conditions prevailing at the time. If it is dead calm, it *may* remain so for the night, but this is unlikely. You will probably get by using long

angled pegs sunk in the snow at a hard angle, but if you suspect that it will be windy, you must use an extra or alternative method. Ice axes, sunk well into the snow make secure anchors for the main load-bearing guys. *Deadmen,* which are rectangular shaped pieces of aluminium used by mountaineers for securing belays, are even better, or, if there is any wood or branches about, select two long staves, roughly the same length as your tent. Tie some cord, or spare guyline around the wood, tie on to your pegging loops, and bury the wood as deeply as possible in the snow, stamping the cover hard on top. This method can also be used using rocks or stones at each individual pegging point. Failing this, stuff-sacks filled with snow make a good alternative. Remember though, that the snow must be stamped down *hard* on top. Then it will freeze and make a strong, secure anchor for the pegs'.

If the weather is really cold, try using ordinary pegs sunk sideways deep in the snow. Pour some water over the top of them and wait for it to freeze. I have often successfully used steel tubes with holes drilled in them. When the peg is driven into the snow, the snow enters the holes and freezes, making a good solid anchor. If the snow is very soft and not too deep then you may be well advised to clear away an area, and pitch directly on to the ground below. If the earth is frozen hard, nick out a hole with the pick end of the ice axe and insert the peg in the softer earth below. A long steel screwdriver can be useful for boring peg holes. Hammer out the holes with this before inserting the softer pegs.

Depending on how hard or soft the snow is, you may find that the tent poles sink into the snow. Some manufacturers of winter tents supply small aluminium discs, which, if inserted underneath the poles, help to prevent them sinking. Such discs can be made from pot lids, small flat stones, bits of wood, the lids from screw top cans or jars, and, if in a real crisis (that is if your poles keep sinking and you have nothing else at all) your boots!

The problem of sinking poles can usually be solved before you pitch the tent, by simply deciding if the consistency of the snow is such that you will be able to camp directly on top of it, or whether, depth permitting, it would

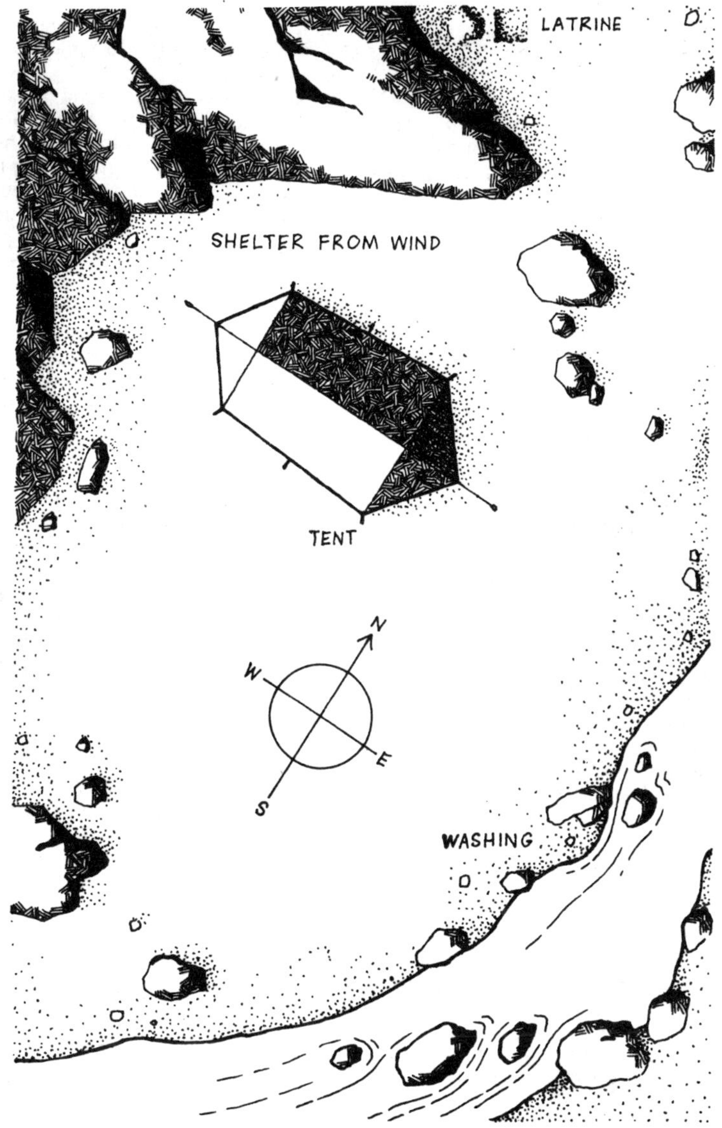

be better to clear an area of snow away and pitch on the firm frozen ground below. Sometimes, though, this causes problems of its own and the pegs won't go in.

All in all, on most occasions, it is best to flatten an area of snow treading it flat and firm, using either the soles of your boots or the flats of skis or both, to tread out the area where the tent will go. As well as making a comfortable surface to sleep on, this also consolidates the snow making it easier to plant pegs and poles.

Once you are well pegged out, erect the poles, and tie on the main load bearing guys, using ice axes or *deadmen,* or whatever, to erect the fly. Get inside, making a last minute check to see that there is nothing on the ground which will penetrate the groundsheet, and clip on the inner. Peg it out and you are ready for that well-deserved brew. The next job is to roll out the insulation mat, pull your sleeping bag out of its stuff-sack, fluff it up and lay it out inside the tent. You can now relax and enjoy the sunset!

SETTLING IN

Once I am in my sleepng bag, cosy and warm, there is nothing, short of an emergency situation which will make me shift out of it until morning. But what about the inevitable result of constant brews? Beside my pillow lies a large plastic bottle clearly marked with a large 'P' in red lettering. When the tent is snug and warm, and the weather outside is cold or wet, this 'P' bottle is luxury. Unfortunately, like so many great pieces of gear, there are pitfalls. The bottle must be of a size which will take your greatest capabilities and sometimes that is difficult to judge!

If the weather is way below zero, and you leave the full bottle until morning before you empty it, you are liable to have a frozen sample. I usually empty mine out the rear of the tent, making certain that no one collects snow for melting from there. Never melt yellow snow!

Other 'nature' calls should be made a fair distance from camp, and it is worth remembering that things stay frozen until the spring thaw, so if possible, dig your latrine, not just in the snow, but in the ground below it. Bury toilet paper as well, it will soon disintegrate in the earth or better still, burn it. All other non-bio-degradable items, like tins, plastic packets and so on, must be carried off the hill and disposed of at home.

Before you finally settle down for the night, or for that matter, immediately after you have pitched your tent and unpacked, have a check around the campsite and make sure nothing is left outside. There is nothing more annoying than to wake in the morning and find half your gear buried from sight below two or three inches of fresh snow and you can lose items like this without great difficulty. Aim to have everything in the shelter of the fly if not inside the main tent with you.

SUB-ZERO NIGHTS

Damp boots will rapidly freeze if left outside, or even in the fly bell of the tent overnight. Putting on frozen boots is one of the most miserable experiences you could imagine, and it takes a good few miles of walking before they begin to thaw out. If the weather is very cold, you may have to take your boots to bed with you, and this will keep them nice and supple till morning. My method is not quite so complicated. I use my boots as a pillow, placing them on their sides, toes pointing out, and putting my shirt and trousers over them. I now have a fairly comfortable pillow, and the boots are protected from the cold. If you don't like the idea of taking your boots to bed with you, and you don't use a pillow, there is another alternative. Bury them! Pop them in a 'poly' bag or stuff-sack, dig a hole in the snow, drop in the bag containing your boots, and cover them up. Remember to mark the spot so that you know where to find them come morning. The snow cover will protect the boots and keep them from freezing too hard. I know people who regularly do this, but it seems a bit severe for me and I like to have my boots handy for any emergency which may occur during the night.

Another bedmate you may have to consider is a plastic or aluminium water bottle. Water will freeze very quickly if left outside, or in the bell of the tent, during sub-zero temperatures, so fill the bottle with enough water to see you through breakfast, and either take it to bed with you, or place it inside the tent wrapped in some article of clothing, between you and your friend. Heat from the sleeping bags should, in all but the more extreme cases, keep the water from freezing. Keep the bottle tilted down so that any ice forms at the bottom and does not clog the neck.

LIVING IN THE SNOW CAMP

Winter camping involves long evenings. If you are the type who is quite happy to lie down and meditate then you will get plenty of opportunity on your winter trips, but campers tend to be energetic people, and lying about for twelve hours or more doing nothing can be a veritable prison sentence. Reading takes up a lot of my time during winter evenings, as this is an activity I don't seem to get a lot of time for at home. Playing cards with your companion, or some other game like chess, or checkers, can eliminate some of the long hours, and cooking huge meals can be fun and most enjoyable. If you and your companion cook on alternate evenings, a good rivalry can be built up as to who can cook the best food, or who can use his culinary skills to change some rather unappetising food into a gastronomic delight. A small radio helps to pass a few hours, but reception is not usually so good in the mountains, although these sets can be useful for receiving weather forecasts. Many mountain areas now have local radio stations which give regular reports on weather, snow and ice conditions and, perhaps the most important, avalanche warnings.

PROBLEMS

Dampness is the big bugbear in snow camping. Bitter cold weather if it is also dry, is exhilarating but higher temperatures and the resultant wet can make life intolerable. The first thing to do is avoid bringing any snow inside the tent. Brush off any snow which has fallen on your clothes before entering the tent. Take your gaiters and boots off at the entrance, and check that the snow is completely cleared from the lace holes or fasteners and from between the lugs on the boot soles. If any snow does get inside the inner tent, and no matter how careful you are some usually does, then brush it out or mop it up as soon as possible. A small sponge, even a small brush, should live beside the tent door at all times for this purpose.

Spindrift is a very fine, dry snow which blows about in the wind, and it is a part of cold weather camping which can virtually make you tear your hair out in frustration. In very cold conditions, this fine powder finds its way into every little crack and niche, and can even penetrate the very fine insect netting in tent doors. If there is a millimetre of space where the tent door zips meet, then you can bet your last dollar that the *spindrift* will come pouring in there. In this type of condition the only thing you can do is lie in wait for it and brush it out before it gets a chance to melt. Spindrift like this is usually a high altitude problem so doesn't affect most of us, but be prepared for it anyway. Dampness will eventually permeate your tent and sleeping bag and that is the time to go off the hill and dry out, using a hut or cabin until your gear is dry and warm again.

WET CLOTHES

No matter what the weather, but the time you have walked a few miles with your pack on, your inner clothes at lest will be damp from perspiration. As soon as you settle in for the night, strip off, put on some dry warm clothing like a 'Polar Suit', and put your damp things in a stuff-sack or 'poly' bag. Some winter campers advocate jumping into your sleeping bag with your perspiration-damp clothes still on, hoping that a warmed-up sleeping bag will be enough to dry off the clothes, but all you will succeed in doing is damping the filling of your sleeping bag. Always keep the inside of the tent as dry as possible. An adequate air flow is essential to give any humid air a chance to escape. Make sure you mop up any liquid spills, or melted snow as quickly as possible.

MATCHES

It is always a good idea to use a lighter for winter camping, as unlike matches they do not suffer from dampness, but, in my experience, lighters are prone to packing up or running out of fuel just when you need them. Gas lighters, like gas stoves, may not ignite in winter. A spare lighter is the answer, or a good supply of matches wrapped up in a watertight container. I normally carry a couple of boxes around in my pocket, but I smoke a pipe so this is habitual. About the only disadvantage in being a non-smoker is that you are liable to forget the matches. Keep some in your food bag all the time, or even better, keep some in your first-aid kit or along with your emergency food. When you are cooking your meal, tuck the box or the lighter somewhere inside your sleeping bag where they will stay dry. It is amazing how quickly a match can become damp in a humid tent, and when the matches won't strike on the box, there's not much chance of them lighting on anything else. Keep them and the striker dry inside a 35mm film canister.

MOVING ON

Getting started again in the morning is another winter problem. It is so nice in the bag.

However you need every hour of daylight so try and get going on a brew and breakfast as soon as the first strip of light shows in the sky.

There will be condensation in the tent and your two objectives must be to:-

1. Pack night clothes and bag away dry.
2. Get dressed and warm yourself without delay.

Both objectives call for a routine. Have your brew and breakfast first from the warmth of the bag. Then rise, dress, in yesterday's clothes, and pack away the bag and night clothes. If it is freezing, loosen the tent from the snow. The warmth inside will have prevented it sticking overnight, but once you get up it can freeze to the snow and if you rip it loose you will eventually destroy the proofing. A space blanket or bivvy bag *under* the tent can prevent this and provide extra insulation.

Pack away all your items of equipment as quickly as possible and be sure to retrieve all pegs covered by the snow. *Check the whole area carefully before you leave it.*

7 · Winter Travel

A winter trip has to be planned. Even a day's walk will be more successful in terms of distance covered and objectives achieved, and the same is even more true if you are intending a longer trip in the winter hills. You must plan, you must check your plan, and you must have other plans available if the first plan doesn't plan out!

Consider and check:-

1. Weather at the time and place.
2. Terrain.
3. Accommodation intended, (tents, huts, snowholes).
4. Distance; is it feasible?
5. Companions; skills and fitness.
6. Possible hazards.
7. Equipment needed.
8. Maps, guides, advice.
9. Back up (support).
10. Alternative plans and escape routes.

You could extend this list almost indefinitely, but the one thing you must do is PLAN. As an experienced three-seasons camper you should not only be able to do this, you should be able to evaluate and judge the worth of your findings and calculations. Above all though, consider the problems of time.

TIME

Moving across the winter landscape, on foot, snow shoe or ski, requires more thought and skill than a summer trip. The hazards are obviously greater and navigation is more difficult. You will more than likely be carrying a heavier pack and weather conditions will be unreliable. All this will affect the timings, and the common error is to allow too little time for the trip.

Speed is far harder to calculate on snow covered terrain. Naismith's Rule (3 mph (4 kph) plus 1 hour for every 2000ft. (650m) climbed) can often be thrown straight out of the window; deep snow drifts, or strong sleeting winds can slow your progress. Even ankle deep snow makes for slow walking. This must be borne in mind when *planning* your winter trip. A mile (say 2km) an hour is good going on snow and try as you will you won't do much more and may do far less. In all your winter trips consider the possible need for escape routes. If the weather turns foul, the snow is too soft or deep, someone becomes frost nipped, or you run out of time, you must get to lower, easier, safer ground quickly. Note on your trip plan the location of huts and shelters, of rescue stations, possible avalanche paths and potential sheltered camp sites. Do this all the time, every time. It's a winter rule.

In the planning stage don't commit yourself to covering too much ground. Remember how short the days are in winter. You may have made a

Sheet no: 184: Start: Farm 896401 Finish: Hill 912442 Mag variation: 8°				
Start	Mag°	Finish	Distance	Time
896401	88°	Barn 909403	2Km	45 mins
909403	48°	Church 916411	1Km (by track)	20 mins
916411	Map	Church 925424	3Km.Rd./F.pth	45 mins
925424	Map	Tumulus 920432	1Km-uphill	30 mins
920432	326°	Hill 912442	1Km	20 mins
	TOTAL	DISTANCE	8Km (5 miles)	160 mins 2 hrs. 40 mins say: 3 hrs.

ROUTE CARD

resolution to start moving at 7 a.m. every morning, but when you look out of the tent door from a warm sleeping bag, and it is still dark and cold outside, there is a great temptation to hang on until daylight cheers the place up a bit. Make allowances for this and for early afternoon camp stops. If you pass a good pitch, sheltered, with running water at 2 p.m. and you reckon you might not find another good pitch until after dark, then stick with the good one, and stop early. It is supposed to be fun!

WALKING IN WINTER

When the snow is crisp and firm, walking on it is no more difficult than it is on firm ground in summer. Start *early* when the snow is frozen. Difficulties arise when the slope becomes steeper and more icy, for a decision must be taken whether to use crampons or not. Generally speaking, crampons can be safely worn in all snow conditions other than soft snow, which balls up between the crampon points and turns your boot sole into an ice skate.

The main difference between summer and winter walking is that winter walking is slower, and one must always be on the lookout for deep soft snow which will bring slow progress to a dead stop. An easy walk out, followed by some fresh snow falls, can become a depressingly slow walk back. The same goes for thaws. A long ski trip out can be great, but if there is a big increase in temperature during the night, then it may well be a case of walking back carrying the skis. These should all be taken into consideration at the *planning stage.* As a general rule, start out early in the day, and walk while the snow is still firm and frozen. Once the sun gets up, your progress will be hard.

Deep wet snow drops the pace to a slow wade, while firm well consolidated snow allows good fast walking, possibly even faster than you would walk in summer. The experienced snow hiker does not just blast headlong in a straight line over the terrain, taking the snow conditions as they come. He searches out the good firm snow if this is at all possible. One side of a ridge may be soft and gooey, while the other side, the side *out of the sun,* may still be hard and firm. Wooded slopes may offer firmer walking than open sunlit slopes, but in certain conditions, it may be the opposite way around. It is virtually impossible to categorise all the conditions and snows, mainly because different areas and times of the year affects the snow to such a degree, but after a while you will begin to know where to find the firmest snow for walking. It's all part of snow appreciation, an art which can only be learned through experience.

Obstacles and dangers along the route should be firmly recognised at the route planning stage. Obviously the avalanche hazard is the main one. Avoid obvious *concave* avalanche slopes and stick to ridges wherever possible. Ask local people where the main avalanche hazards exist and be sure to stay well clear.

KEEPING WARM AND DRY

The major problem in snow travel is keeping warm and dry. Walking, skiing and snow shoeing are all fairly strenuous activities, and you will be warm, maybe even hot, while on the move but, as soon as you stop, for a snack or a rest, you will rapidly cool down. Many people will tell you that it is dangerous to sweat in winter conditions. This may be so, but you try telling your body that as you struggle up a steep ridge with a 40lb pack on your back! Try to balance heat production and heat loss by proper use of zips, putting on the really warm and windproof clothing at rest stops when chilling will take place within minutes. Have your cagoule strapped to the *outside* of your pack for just this reason. If it's handy you will slip into it and so stay warm.

Keeping dry is another problem. If snow is falling, you will be better to wear smooth-surfaced fabrics like proofed nylon from which the flakes will slide off before they get a chance to melt. Brush off any snow which begins to accumulate on your clothing, but beware that snow, melting off the cagoule, does not soak your trousers. Knock snow from tree branches before you pass under them, for your pack may catch them and dump snow on top of you. In winter, remember the 'wind-chill' factor (see Hazards chapter).

TRAIL FOODS AND WATER

Eat plenty of carbohydrate loaded food as you walk along. Chocolate, boiled sweets, glucose sweets, all help to maintain body warmth and energy. Keep well topped up with liquids. If the streams are frozen over, chew some snow, or suck ice, letting it melt in your mouth before swallowing. Carry the water bottle *upside down* in a pocket of your pack so that any ice which forms cannot plug the neck, and, if the weater is really cold, stick the bottle inside a sock, or wrap it up in a sweater, anything to try and stop it freezing. Try and drink warm liquids, like tea, rather than cold water which requires body heat to warm it, or even coffee which is a diuretic and reduces your body water.

DANGER

Be careful when you are walking near trees or rocks, as the trunks, or isolated rocks, being warmer than the surrounding snow, will melt deep pits around them. This can be awkward if you fall in! Snow is usually softer and deeper near trees and rocks and on at least one side of walls, as the result of the 'lee' such objects provide to driving snow.

SNOW BRIDGES

More obvious dangers include stream crossings and snow bridges over streams or crevasses. A collapsing snow bridge can dump you into very cold rushing water, often swift enough to carry you downstream into snow tunnels. If you *must* cross a snow bridge, make sure it is a good thick stable one, and only expose one member of the party at a time. Undo your hip belt in case you have to get rid of your pack in a hurry, and position other party members downstream in case they have to pull you out. Probe the bridge in front of you as you cross with a ski pole or ice axe.

Rivers which freeze over deeply in winter often present a special hazard in springtime. As the break-up is approaching, the ice, which is thick, becomes very unstable, and forms long vertical crystals known as 'candle ice'. Ice like this is not capable of supporting very much weight. It is better to stay off iced-up rivers in the spring, especially when there is an overflow of water on top of the ice, for it is often difficult to calculate how deep the water actually is, and this water will certainly weaken the ice.

Streams and rivers always present problems. Wide rivers in winter should only be crossed by bridges. In mountain areas, large rivers run very, very cold, and sudden immersion could very well result in hypothermia, so don't risk it. Another point to remember is that frozen rivers have very uneven layers of ice. You might manage to tip-toe across three quarters of the width of the river before it decides to crack open, toppling you into the water below. If the water is flowing at any speed at all, you are liable to be swept under the ice to a cold, wet grave.

In these situations it is wise to use a rope, one person crossing the ice, or snow bridge at a time, while securely belayed by a partner.

Lakes usually freeze up firmer than rivers, and can often give good firm, safe highway, but watch out for the points where streams or rivers flow into the lake as this usually results in a thinning of the ice layer. Other thin spots usually occur near the shoreline.

Beware of snow bridges across streams in the late afternoon, or when the temperature suddenly rises. It is also a good point to remember that snow overhangs a stream almost like a cornice. Add the weight of an unsuspecting walker and the overhang could well topple you into the icy water. This is worth remembering when you are not attempting to cross but just going there for water.

WALKING ACROSS SLOPES

When traversing snow slopes, dig the side of your boot into the slope so that it forms its own platform. If you place your boot at the same angle as the slope, it will just slide downhill, like a skier side-slipping. The same goes for descending snow slopes. Dig the heels in, preferably with the heels lower than the toes, so that the sole will support your weight without slipping.

HUTS

This may be a book on snow *camping,* but don't discount the use of bothies or huts. On an extended trip in countries like France or Norway, in the U.S.A. or Canada, and in most mountain regins, you may want to stay in a hut for a night if you come across one, if only to get a good fire going and dry off some gear. Many areas are unsuitable for camping and snow travellers rely on huts. Huts come in all shapes and sizes, from the most basic stone shelter to a real backwood log cabin complete with stone fireplace with a stag's head above it and a guitar hanging on the wall. These places can be an oasis in the wilderness to many people, and it is a good idea to check them out *on the map* at the planning stages of your trip. They are especially useful in an emergency. Youth hostels also come into this category, although for some inexplicable reason most hostels close down during the winter months, although really remote hostels usually have some outbuilding which is kept open for emergency use.

If you use a hut, do try and leave it cleaner and tidier than it was when you found it. Someone, somewhere, will be responsible for the hut, so consider him or her if you are tempted to throw rubbish around. If a hut gets into a real mess continually, sooner or later the person who owns it, or looks after it, will close it down and then we all lose out because of an inconsiderate few. If you have any spare food on your last day, consider leaving it behind as hut stores, for the benefit of some less well organized visitor.

CLUBS

Winter travel in the hills is an expanding activity, and more and more huts are staying open or being built to cater for it — or for us.

Membership of the Y.H.A., the Norwegian D.N.T., the Club Alpin Français, the Austrian Alpine Club, or such American organizations as the Adirondack Mountain Club, is useful if you want to use these huts. The fees are less, the information you receive more up to date and your fees help the club to carry on the good work. No non-member is ever turned away but non-members cannot book ahead and will pay higher hut charges.

ROUTE CARDS AND PARTY TRAVEL

Finally, before you leave, and then again every day, spend some time in the tent at night or first thing in the morning estimating bearings and times. Make out your *'route card'* for the day in the comfort of a sleeping bag, rather than on a hill top with a Force Eight blowing. There is less chance of making mistakes doing it this way. Always have your calculations checked by your companion.

When travelling in a group, appoint a 'back marker' to keep the group together. This is an especially good idea in 'white-outs' to make sure that you do not lose contact. The back marker should also check the leader's navigation as the party moves along. If conditions get so bad that you cannot make out landmarks, then put someone out in front and take the bearing on him. Tell him to move right or left, or whatever is necessary to get him in line with your compass needle, before you move up and repeat the process but make sure he doesn't get so far in front that he loses contact, or gets out of earshot.

When you are traversing, there is a tendency to lose height, or, if you become aware of this, a tendency to over-correct the opposite way. Use the compass constantly in poor visibility.

Deep snow brings its own problems, especially in estimating time, so it may be worth while keeping to ridges where the snow is usually blown clear. Easier going will also be found on windward slopes. Beware at all times though of avalanche risk, especially under cornices and ice slopes.

LEAVE A NOTE OF YOUR ROUTE

This should be an automatic procedure even on summer trips, but in winter it is even more important. The dangers are greater, navigation is more difficult, and the consequences of getting lost are more serious. Leave a note with a respnsible person, and don't be content with a bit of paper on your car windscreen. If it snows heavily it is possible for your car to be covered, so your note might not be found until days after you should have returned. You are also giving thieves notice that they have time to rob your car. Leave your note with the Police, a reliable friend or a warden or ranger. Be sure you let them know when you return or you may start a quite unnecessary search.

Common sense plays a big part in winter travel. The finest piece of gear you carry is perched between your ears. Use it well, think in advance, and consider any dangers before they occur — then avoid them.

8 · Skis and Snow Shoes

Given snow, and the right equipment, you can travel long distances in a short winter day. The right equipment consists of Nordic skis. With snow shoes you can stay mobile in the softest, deepest snow, and some knowledge of skiing and snow shoeing is essential for the committed snow camper.

WINTER RUCKSACK FEATURES

There is no real reason why your usual summer sac can't be used for most winter work, providing it is large enough, say 60 litres or more, to carry the extra winter gear like bigger or bulkier sleeping bags, more clothing, and heavier tents. It should, however, have certain in-built features. Ice axe and crampon attachment points are useful and ski pockets or straps are necessary for the ski tourer. It is worthwhile bearing in mind that very few sacs available today are truly waterproof. Pack all your gear into 'poly' bags or nylon stuff sacks before putting them inside the pack. A wet sleeping bag is a most miserable companion during a cold winter night.

The bottom of the sac will often rest in the snow and anything kept there will need extra protection. Check also that the pockets have good closure flaps to stop spindrift blowing on to the contents.

If you go ski touring you may need to change your sac. The ideal XC sac has no side pockets, is frameless or with a light integral frame and has both hip harness and sternum straps. You should load your sac for ski-ing with the heaviest items at the bottom to help balance.

Side pockets will inhibit the arm action necessary for XC skiing. A framed sac will tend to overbalance the skier on the turn and extra straps help the sack to fit firmly to the skier's back and aid balance. That said, many Nordic skiers use frame sacs or even pack frames. It is just harder to ski with them.

Now let's look at skis.

CROSS COUNTRY SKIING

Langlauf, ski-de-fond, cross country, ski touring, Nordic skiing, XC or ski-packing — the nomenclature is unimportant — all mean much the same thing.

Ski touring is now booming as never before, and rightly so, for it offers a fast, easy and extremely enjoyable way of exploring the back country in the depths of winter.

All you need for a successful ski tour is winter backpacking gear, some ankle deep snow and suitable cross-country skis, poles, bindings and boots, plus, of course, a grasp of XC technique. The Scandinavians were happy to use the same type of wooden ski for centuries, but the recent growth in the sport has led to much change and variety, or indeed resulted from it. Touring skis now come in many different lengths and widths, are made of different materials including a wide range of synthetics, and have different running surfaces, some of which need waxing and others which manage to do without it.

At one end of the scale is the light racing *langlauf* ski, long and slim for the prepared racing track, the thoroughbred competition ski but not suitable for our purpose. At the other end comes the steel-edged *mountain* ski, a close relative of the modern downhill piste ski. Somewhere in between these two comes the *general touring* ski, the ideal tool for ski touring or snow camping. A ski which is between 4.5lb (2 kilos) and 6lb (2.5 kilos) in weight, between 52mm and 60mm in width at the binding, with whole or half steel edges, is the one to look for.

Laminated wooden skis with 'lignostone' edges, a substance formed from compressed beech, were, until recently, the most popular touring ski, but modern technology has brought the advantage of fibreglass, polyethelene, and polyurethane (PU). These skis unquestionably offer great advantages in weight and strength, important considerations when backcountry skiing.

BUYING XC SKIS

The correct length of ski can be measured by holding the ski vertically beside you. Stretch your arm above your head, and if the ski is the correct length the tip will reach your wrist. The skis should have enough curve or 'camber' to support your weight with a loaded pack, without the tips leaving the snow. You can check the camber by placing the skis together, base to base and trying to snap them together with one hand. If it is too easy the skis are too soft; too hard, and they are too stiff. If you can do it with effort the skis are about right.

The most popular general touring skis are made in fibreglass laminate. Fibreglass is light and tough, and the treated polyethelene or PU base is much easier to maintain than the traditional wood. A minimum of fuss is what the ski tourer is after, and a great performance in terms of speed is not generally demanded. With a thirty pound pack on your back, it is quite difficult to maintain the traditional explosive action of the Nordic skier, so the heavier than usual, broad-based, steel-edged ski suits the purpose admirably.

WAXING OR NOT?

For the best performance in any type of cross country ski, it is usually necessary to wax the bottoms for *grip* and *glide.* The only exception to this is the *non-wax* ski. These skis are a fairly new innovation and have caught on well among those who don't particularly need a high performance from their skis. Most ski tourers will find non-wax skis perfectly adequate. The heavy load makes proper technique difficult, although good technique greatly reduces the effort involved in XC skiing. Even so, a little wax on ski tip and tail helps to speed you along. Overall though, go for a non-wax ski.

NON-WAX SKIS

There are various types of non-wax ski. Some have a plastic *fish scale* base which is an overlapping pattern of discs stamped into the sole, just like fish scales. Another type has diamond patterns, while *step-cut* skis and the type with strips of mohair set in the base on either side of the centre groove are also available. All these bases allow you to climb slopes without sliding backwards. The mohair or the serrations *grip* the snow when pushed

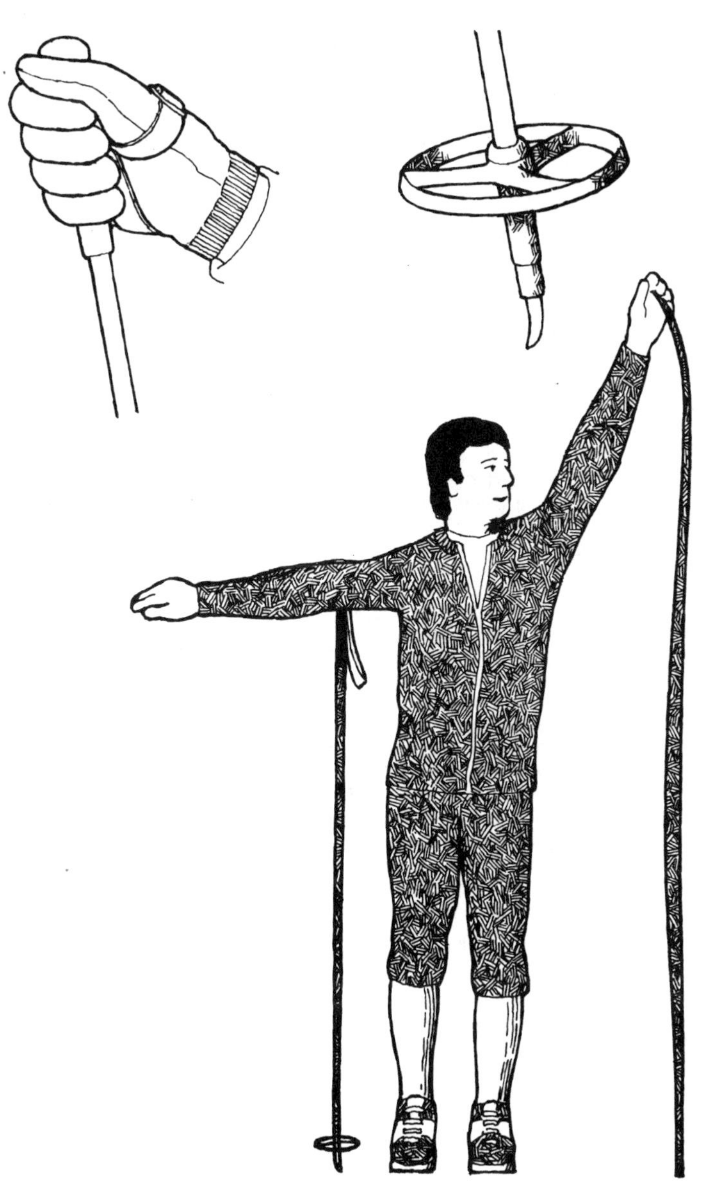

backwards, but allow the skier to glide forward. This, although with some loss in performance, gives a similar effect to the waxable ski.

However, if you do want to wax, let me not stand in your way.

WAX

The purpose of wax is to provide 'grip' between the bottom of the ski and the snow when pushed backwards, while allowing the ski to glide forward over the snow without sticking. Waxing is something which confuses many people, but it is really quite simple. If you look at snow through a magnifying glass, you will see that it has a very rough surface. The waxed ski surface also presents a rough and irregular face, depending on which type of wax you have rubbed on. These surfaces bind together to provide grip, but when the snow is compressed it melts and with the friction of a kick forward, you travel on, gliding on a layer of melted water.

Most wax manufacturers list on the package the type of wax to be used in a given snow condition, 'fresh snow', 'old snow', 'below freezing' and so on, which makes the choice of wax much easier. There are basically three types of wax; hard, soft and klister. All are colour coded, ranging usually from green wax for fresh sub-zero temperatures to red klister, a soft sticky wax for old, wet, melting snow. If this sounds difficult, then there are 'wide range waxes' which work on either wet (above zero) or dry (below zero) snow states, and limit your decisions to one. Is it above or below freezing.

Waxing is not something to worry about. It can even be an art and many of the traditionalists derive as much pleasure from their knowledge of waxing as they do from skiing itself. If you decide to try waxed skis, begin with a few waxes from one manufacturer; watch which kind of waxes others are using, ask questions and learn as you go. Even non-wax skis work better with a little wax, so some knowledge of waxing is always useful.

POLES

Cross country poles should be long enough to fit under the armpits, like crutches. Basically the poles are the simplest part of the ski tourer's outfit and are made of Tonkin bamboo, aluminium or fibre glass. Cross country poles have wide snap-on baskets, adjustable wrist straps, and tips which curve forward for easy placement and removal from the snow.

BOOTS

Ski touring boots, come in a variety of shapes and styles. The cross-country racer uses very lightweight training shoe type boots, cut below the ankle, like a running shoe, but the tourer needs boots cut above the ankle with a sewn-in tongue, a snow collar at the ankle, and a proofed leather upper. As the tourer moves along most of the day with a sliding action, it is imperative that the boot he uses is pliable enough to bend at the sole, but without side play. XC boots bend forward easily but have a metal instep flange to prevent laterial distortion. It is important that the boot is compatible with the type of binding on the ski, and most are now made to the 75 *Nordic Norm.* New types of binding, such as the 50mm *Touring Norm* are coming in so be careful when making your choice. A backcountry touring boot should be reasonably waterproof. Long gaiters or 'stop tous' help to keep the snow out, and it is also possible to buy 'boot gloves' which are waterproof and do a good job in keeping the feet dry.

BINDINGS

Touring ski bindings only grip the toe of the boot so that the heel may rise up and down as it would when walking.

Pin type bindings are commonly used on touring skis. These bindings attach to the toe of the boot with a 'mouse-trap' type clamp which presses the toe of the boot down into little pins which mate into holes in the boot toe. The toe is held firm, but the heel can lift when necessary. These pin bindings come in various sizes, the most common at present being the 75mm Nordic Norm. You must be careful that the pins in the binding are compatible with the holes in the boot sole., *Rottefella* bindings are just one good make.

Pin bindings are fine for touring, or general touring over moderate terrain, but if you want to head for the hills, then you might consider the cable binding, like the *Tempo.* A metal cable runs behind the heel and holds the toe of the boot in a toepiece. Some of these cable bindings have fitments which allow the cable to be clamped to the ski, rather like a downhill type binding, but unfortunately without a quick release. This allows greater control in downhill running, but the risk of injury if you fall when running downhill with a heavy pack is quite considerable.

TECHNIQUE

If you have never done any XC skiing before, don't worry. The basic ski touring techniques are almost as simple as walking. The basic movement is called the *diagonal stride,* an easy, uncomplicated movement over the snow in a gliding action. The diagonal stride has two phases, the 'kick', and the 'glide'. These movements are supported by strong swinging forward-and-back actions of the arms and poles.

As you slide one foot forward, the opposite arm also swings forward. Plant the forward pole in the ground, slanting to the rear, and as the other leg swings through, give yourself a push off the rear leg. Keep pushing off one ski on to the other, resting your weight and balance on the forward ski and let it slide until it almost stops. Repeat, pushing off the rear ski on to the other which is thrust forward and allowed to slide. This 'glide' and 'kick' comes with a little practise, and if you ever get the chance to see an experienced ski tourer in action you will clearly see this explosive kicking action followed by the relaxed glide phase, a beautiful technique to watch when properly executed.

There are many good books on the subject and *'Ski Touring'* by Rob Hunter, which is also published in this Master Guide Series, or the Venture Guide *'Cross Country Skiing'* will tell you all you need to know. There is quite a lot to learn, and although the techniques are simple, they will only develop effectively with practise.

If ski touring intrigues you, read as much as possible about it, and enrol in a training course if there is one available near you.

Ski touring on XC skis is an excellent way of travelling the backcountry in winter. Just give it a try and you will soon become a convert.

SNOW SHOES

While cross country skis have undergone tremendous development in the past few years, the snow shoe is still much the same as it was when the American Indians used them for hunting in winter time.

Let me list the advantages of snow shoes.

1. Snow shoeing is easy to learn. A mere five minutes is all it takes to adjust your gait to allow for the extra width of the shoe. This is a big advantage for the camper who is suddenly faced with deep powder snow. If he can get a hold of some snow shoes he can soon be on his way, learning the finer points of technique as he walks along.
2. Almost any boot designed for walking can be used with snow shoes, unlike skis where a special boot must be used to fit the ski binding. This saves trouble and expense.
3. Snow shoes are probably better than skis in closely wooded country or where the snow is patchy and inconsistent and manoeuvrability is of prime importance.
4. If, for any reason, you have to take off your snow shoes, because of steep slopes, snow shoes are easier to carry than skis, and you don't need to carry poles as well, although some people do.

Despite these advantages, snow shoeing is a slow way to travel, and the thrills and exhilaration of XC skiing are missing. They are, however, a practical sort of footwear, and deserve more consideration from winter hikers and snow campers than they usually get.

Traditionally the framing is of some type of varnished wood, the webbing made from rawhide thong, although modern snow shoes often have neoprene webbing and an aluminium frame. Beware of plastic framed snow shoes! Part of my lack of enthusiasm for snow shoes stems from an experience of cheap plastic ones which broke and left me floundering in deep snow some considerable miles from base.

There are many different snow shoe designs, one for almost every snow condition, but the main thing is to use one with sufficient surface area to support your weight over the snow, which for a camper means the snow shoe plus whatever weight he carries. It is tiring to wear a snow shoe which is too small, as you will sink in fairly deeply with each step, but wearing one which is too large is equally tiring. Most manufacturers list the exact size and capacity of each of their models, so it isn't too difficult to find a pair which will suit you, but remember to include the weight of the pack in your estimate.

Of the smaller snow shoes, the most popular and widely used, tend to be the *'bear paw'* design. These are typically 8-12 inches wide and up to 30 inches long. They have a rounded toe, swept slightly upward, and a rounded tail. Shoes which extend to a narrow tail at the back are called *'beavertails'*. The *'Yukon'* style has a long narrow upswept toe, and is used mainly for breaking trail in powder snow. A pair of small *'racquettes'* made with an aluminium frame and neoprene webbing is adequate for moving around the campsite. They weigh little and can be carried in your rucksack until needed.

When the snow is soft, you can climb quite steep slopes simply by kicking the shoes firmly into the slope. On hard snow or icy slopes, you will slip, and would be well advised to take the snow shoes off and walk, although you can buy snow shoe 'crampons' which fit on the bottom of the shoes and allow you to negotiate icy slopes fairly securely.

SNOW SHOE BINDINGS

The foot is attached to the snow shoe by means of a binding which, when the foot is raised to step forward, will allow the tail of the snow shoe to drop down and the toe flip upward. When you wear a snow shoe your boot rests on webbing attached near the toe to a stout crossbar. There should be no webbing immediately in front of this crossbar.

You need the type of binding which will allow your foot to be firmly attached to the snow shoe without permitting any side twisting of the shoe. The best bindings are also those which will allow you to attach and buckle the snow shoe to the boot easily, a great boon when your hands are stiff and cold. Canvas strips are durable but get very stiff when wet and cold, so choose neoprene.

HINTS ON SNOW SHOEING

1. When starting to walk on snow shoes take it slowly and easily. Look around you, relax, and stay relaxed, and avoid rushing.
2. Take long natural steps. Don't straddle your legs and only pick up your foot high enough to clear the other shoe. Most beginners straddle along with their legs wide apart lifting their feet too high, which is very tiring and will lead to falls.
3. If you are having problems with balance, get some ski poles for extra support.
4. Don't try and reverse, or back up ever! The tails of the snow shoes will stick into the snow and you will topple over backwards! It can't be done; you have to circle round.
5. Small is beautiful. Don't be tempted into buying a shoe which is too large for you under the impression that it will 'float' better on soft snow. You will just find them too awkward for easy manoeuvrability and the right size for your weight will suit all situations.
6. Dry snow shoes at room temperature but not in front of direct heat. Direct heat will cause the webbing to become brittle, and depending on the frame, may cause delamination in the shoe itself.

I have only described skiing and snow shoeing briefly in this chapter. To cover them in every detail would require a volume on its own, and there is already such a book in this series — *'Ski Touring'* which covers the subject in detail.

However, you cannot call yourself a complete snow camper until you have a good grasp of XC ski and snow shoe techniques. Both techniques are easy to learn and will add immensely to your outdoor opportunities.

9 · Snow and Snow Holes

The snow camper, by definition, will live and travel in the winter landscape and therefore goes into the wilds at a critical time of the year. For much of the time, common sense, good gear, and limited objectives will reward you with a great deal of fun in complete security. However . . .

When the winter weather turns foul you cannot fight it head on. You must bend, and adapt yourself to the conditions using the snow and the elements, however savage, to help you stay alive.

In this chapter, then, let us study snow, and how to live in and with it.

SNOW

Snow reaches the earth in millions of tiny, beautifully shaped crystals, which as snowfall follows snowfall eventually accumulates on the ground in layers. The density of this falling snow depends on air temperature as well as crystal type and there can be several types of snow in one fall. The lightest snow falls under cold dry conditions. The highest densities are associated with *graupel* (soft hail) or 'needle crystals' which fall at temperatures near freezing point.

As soon as the snowflakes land, they begin a process of change known as *metamorphism.* The crystals break down, the complex forms are rounded off and the feathery crystals become a mass of globules. This metamorphism is a continuous process which begins at the time the snow lands on the ground and carries on until it eventually melts. Metamorphism is caused by a transfer of vapour from the points of the crystals to the more central parts. The snow crystal itself is reduced in size but becomes more dense. Add weight of newly fallen snow above and the effects of a strong wind, (which can penetrate even thick masses of snow), and you can see why a foot of snow can be reduced to eight inches or so after a few days, without actually melting. This is known as *destructive metamorphism,* a confusing phrase as the snow is actually being consolidated.

This settling of the snow allows the crystals to bond together and form a better cohesion between the various layers of snow, but the bonding of crystals inside any one layer (that is the layer of crystals which have fallen at the same time) is stronger than the bonding between distinct layers of snow (those layers which fell at different times and are of a different consistency). This difference is the major cause of snow's inherent instability.

Next follows a process called *constructive metamorphism.* This is caused when water vapour is transferred from one part of the snow layer to another by vertical diffusion. This vapour migration causes a reduction in both the texture and the cohesion of the lower layers so that the whole snow cover is weakened from within. The vapour continues its upward travel, until it is re-deposited as ice on a higher level of crystals, and builds them up in size until they become large cup-shaped crystals (cup crystals) with very poor adhesion qualities. These cup crystals are the most common cause of avalanches.

In warmer climates, *constructive metamorphism* leads to a general toughening of the upper layers of the snow cover, at the expense of the lower layers. In very cold temperatures *depth hoar* is formed in the lower regions of the snow cover. This depth hoar dividing the snowfall layers is potentially dangerous, as it forms a very fragile base for the layers above. The danger is heightened by the fact that this type of metamorphism can take place at any depth in the layers of snow, and is likely to remain undetected unless the depth of the snow cover is examined in a sunken pit, (or the slope avalanches). The surface layers can appear perfectly stable, and give no indication of the danger lurking below. Because of this poor adhesion between the layers of snow, constructive metamorphism, and the resulting cup crystals, can have a direct bearing on later avalanches. Such conditions, while possible at any time, are most common in early winter when the snow cover is shallow and still unconsolidated, and late in the season when the consolidated snow is starting to melt.

As snow campers, instability in snow is of major importance, for snow is our medium of travel and our home, and we have to rely on it. Unstable snow which will not take our weight, soft snow which makes walking akin to wading or packed ice which makes skiing impossible, are all inevitable at some time. Unstable snow, which is likely to avalanche, is less probable, but always in inherent danger. Snow, therefore, is both a friend and an enemy, and which one it is at any one time depends on the climate and the snow state.

SNOW TYPES

There are certain basic types of snow which you will learn to recognise. Fresh snow is no help to us. It gives little support, especially if it is the light 'powder' variety. Old and wet snow has a bluish tinge, is unpleasant to walk on and can easily avalanche. Old powder snow has a greyish tinge and has a crust, which is often formed over powder snow by freezing winds. *Neve,* or *Skare,* is old hard snow, which has been melted and refrozen time and time again. This is fine for walking on but hard for skiing. Neve, however, will adhere to steep slopes and makes first class winter walking conditions.

SNOW HOLES

The insulating properties of snow are well known. Scientists at the University of Colorado have made comparisons between snow and down, in terms of insulation. In both, the major insulating agent consists of millions of tiny, trapped dead-air pockets. In down, these dead-air pockets are formed between the particles of the feathers and in snow exactly the same thing happens in the piling and interlocking of the snowflakes. Small birds and mammals survive well in snowy winters, protected against the wind in the shelter of snowy banks and hedges.

A fresh layer of snow may hold from 60 to 90 percent air, depending upon its structure. Once snow has been on the ground for a time, the shapes of the snowflakes change; the sharp points and edges disappear and the once beautiful flakes become a compact mass, but much of the original trapped air remains. The old snow may not hold as much air but what it does hold is more effectively trapped, and the insulation qualities of the snow actually improve.

Once you dig a hole into this compact snow, you effectively insulate yourself in much the same way as you do when you crawl into a sleeping bag. The original temperature of the snow trapped air is near the average air temperature at the time the snow fell, but very soon body heat, and the heat from candles and stoves produces a considerable change inside the snow hole. Due to these heat sources, the air temperature in the snow hole starts rising towards freezing point, even when it is well below zero outside.

The temperature inside the snow cave should be kept around freezing point, so as to avoid drips from melting snow. Freezing point may not sound very comfortable, but it is far superior to a humid, mushy, dripping wet snow cave at higher temperatures. To appreciate the comfort level of freezing point, all you have to do is stick your nose out of the snow hole into the night air, where the wind and cold temperatures outside make the snow hole feel like a centrally heated flat!

SNOW HOLING EQUIPMENT

To make a real fast workmanlike job of your snow cave or snow hole, snow shovels and even a snow saw are necessary. Before I go any further let me add that I personally know of few winter backpackers who set off equipped with these items, unless they have the definite intention of living in a cave or igloo. However, if you intend travelling really lightweight, or using a snow cave as some form of base, then get yourself a broad short handled shovel, and a small large toothed saw. These tools don't weigh too much, and there are specially designed snow shovels which allow the handle to fold over the spade; the *Witco* shovel is excellent.

I carry a shovel and saw when I am teaching someone how to build a snow cave, or to give them some experience in living in a snow hole, but generally, all I use is an ice axe, my feet and hands, and in some cases a pot or pan lid.

BUILDING A SNOW HOLE

Apart from the emergency aspect of snow caves used when caught out in

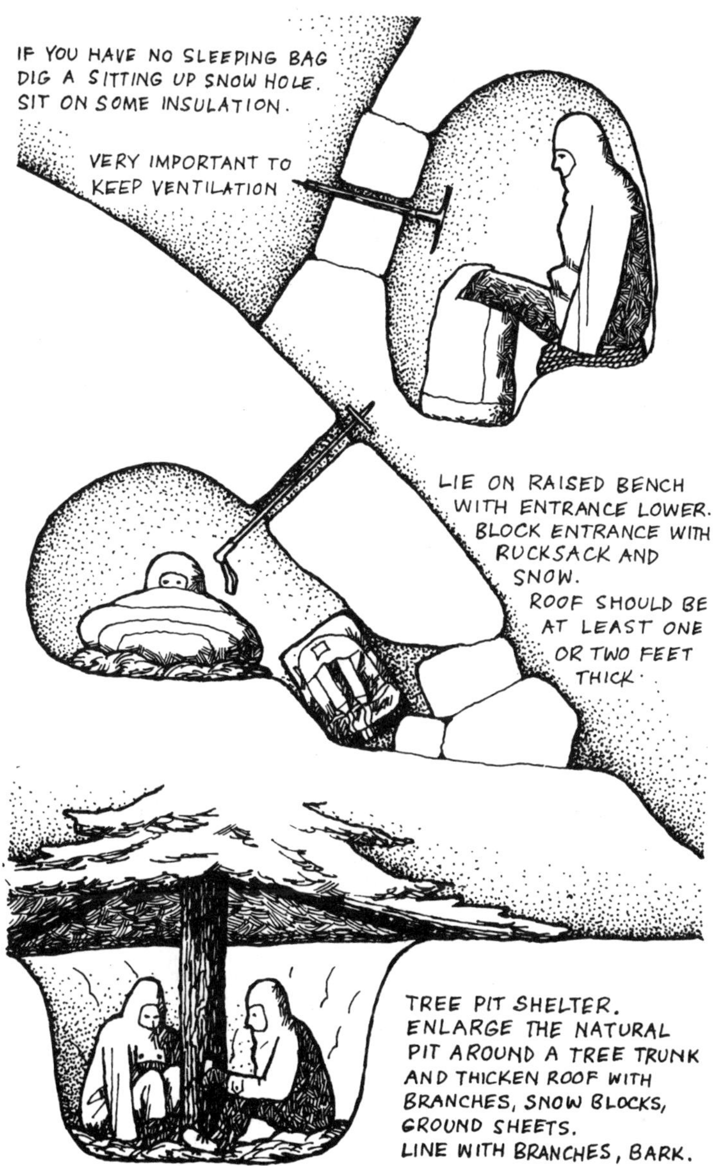
IF YOU HAVE NO SLEEPING BAG
DIG A SITTING UP SNOW HOLE.
SIT ON SOME INSULATION.
VERY IMPORTANT TO
KEEP VENTILATION
LIE ON RAISED BENCH
WITH ENTRANCE LOWER.
BLOCK ENTRANCE WITH
RUCKSACK AND
SNOW.
ROOF SHOULD BE
AT LEAST ONE
OR TWO FEET
THICK.
TREE PIT SHELTER.
ENLARGE THE NATURAL
PIT AROUND A TREE TRUNK
AND THICKEN ROOF WITH
BRANCHES, SNOW BLOCKS,
GROUND SHEETS.
LINE WITH BRANCHES, BARK.

the winter hills without a tent, or when conditions are so bad that pitching a tent would be tempting fate, a night in a snow hole often makes a luxurious departure from the normal cramped existence of winter camping in a small tent. Just to be able to stand up, move about, and get off your belly for a while makes all the effort worthwhile. The only drawback is that cave building takes a fair amount of effort. Two hours per man is about average time for a good snow hole, sufficient to accommodate a group of walkers. So four or five hours will build a super cave for two, complete with kitchen and bedroom. Building a hole like this is a bit like building sandcastles on the beach. Once you have the basic shelter, some impulse tempts you on to building more and more, until time, energy, or both, run out.

The choice of the type of snow shelter to build, cave, hole or igloo is more or less dependent upon the terrain and the prevailing snow conditions. Other factors to be considered are the experience of the party, the time available, and the urgency of the situation. By far my favourite, and possibly the most reliable in terms of structural strength, is the snow cave.

THE SNOW CAVE

For this you need a deep, firm snow drift which is not exposed to avalanches or below cornices. Snow which is good for snow holing is also good for avalanching. Test the depth and consistency of the snow with the ice axe or ski pole. A snow cave consists of a dome hollowed out in the snow bank, big enough for two people to lie stretched out and almost high enough to stand upright. Before you start work, strip off any extra clothing you are wearing. Cave building is very hot work, and if you soak your clothing with sweat or melting snow, it is quite likely it will freeze up again during the night.

Dig a slot into the drift, wide enough for easy entry, and high enough to work in comfortably. Although the final entrance should be quite small, don't worry about that at this stage, as it can be filled in with snow later on. A small folding spade comes in handy here, but this is really only worthwhile on longer trips when you are certain of finding suitable conditions or as a safety item, or when you definitely intend living in a snow hole. I usually break up the snow with the adze of the ice axe, kick fallen snow on to my insulating mat, and use that as a sledge to pull the excess snow clear. Once this snow is outside, my companion shapes it into blocks to be used later in the entrance tunnel.

Dig into the bank for about up to 3 metres. Once in this far you have the basis of your shelter. Then, working from the back, start enlarging the cave. Make it big enough for two people to lie stretched out, tall enough to stand upright or just in a crouch. Remembering that warm air rises, so build a couple of platforms into the walls as sleeping benches and make sure you will be sleeping at a higher level than the top of the entrance tunnel. Once you have built a fairly generous cavern, with the roof and walls smoothed down to prevent drip points forming, start filling in the entrance with the snowballs or snow blocks. Fill the entrance in completely, and then dig the entry tunnel out through the bottom. You only need enough space to crawl through. Do not make the cave excessively large. It may seem nice but it will be colder than a smaller one.

Finally, make a ventilation hole in the roof. This is important, as nearly all the recorded accidents in snow shelters have been caused by carbon monoxide poisoning from stoves. If you find yourself with the beginnings of a headache immediately after, or during cooking, you had better do something about increasing ventilation — and quickly. A flickering and smoking candle flame is another early indicator of monoxide in the air or a lack of oxygen.

It is essential to leave the door open all the time and check that it isn't blocked up by drifting snow outside. Always ventilate the cave, and especially when cooking.

Once safely established inside the cave, you can begin enlarging your home. Cut small shelves in the walls for cooking, storing food or placing candles. Place 'poly' bags or insulation mats on the floor for carpets; form well shaped bed benches with built-in pillows for sleeping and have one corner of the cave kept aside for cutting snow for water. If you leave the cave for any length of time, make certain that it is well marked. There have been quite a few recorded instances of walkers wandering the hillside in the middle of the night searching in vain for their snow cave. A drifted-over cave looks just like any other snow drift. It is a good idea to mark the top of the cave with an ice axe or flag it using a ski pole with a scarf tied to it. This not only enables you to find your cave again, but it also stops people dropping in for dinner unannounced!

One safety point. *Always bring your ice axe, snow shovel or digging implements into and out of the cave with you.* You may well find the entrance tunnel filling up with snow and you may have to dig your way out or in again.

IGLOOS

A very good type of shelter in suitable snow conditions is a hybrid between the snow cave and the igloo. This is built when you can only find a shallow drift, not deep enough for a full scale cave, but big enough for a small shelter. Dig into the drift as for the cave until you run out of snow, and then start cutting blocks to form the front section of the shelter. Using this method you can build as far outwards as you like, so that say, half the shelter is a snow cave and the rest is formed from the excavated blocks, a demi-igloo.

The pure igloo can take a fair bit of time to build, but offers in the end a solid, structurally sound, shelter, which will remain standing for a long time, even during a thaw. The problem with igloo building is that the snow must have the right consistency. New unconsolidated snow which can be packed and allowed to harden is ideal, but this is hard work and takes time.

Wet snow can be rolled into huge snowballs, and then cut into blocked shapes, but even a small igloo takes a lot of rolling and this is very hard work. You need snow which is hard enough to take your weight when standing on it without snow shoes or skis. The snow should have the same consistency throughout the block and not just be crusted on top. A snow saw, or a spade is really necessary for igloo building.

Select your site, again well away from potential avalanche paths though your choice of site will probably be dictated by the source of building snow. Mark out a circle in the snow and dig out a shallow pit. The size of the igloo will depend on how many people intend sleeping in it, but as a general rule allow say 3 metres diameter for two or three people. With one person cutting out blocks, the other can do the actual building. Stand inside the pit, and place the blocks round the circumference in an inward leaning spiral. The larger the blocks, the quicker you will build the igloo. Build gradually upwards, remembering to camber the blocks so that they are always leaning inwards. As the building nears completion, you will find it difficult to pass the blocks out to one another, so a 'window' must be cut out in the side so that the blocks can be passed to the person.

When the final block, the keystone in the roof, is due to be put in place, pass it through the remaining space end on, and then lower it gently into position. Smooth off all the walls, plastering the outside with snow and pass any surplus snow out through your window before sealing it up. If you are really lucky, you might be able to find a piece of thick ice to put in the window space instead of sealing it. Finally, burrow out the door, and build a short entrance tunnel. Remember to poke out a couple of ventilation holes in the roof. The door should be built at right angles to the prevailing wind to prevent snow drifting in. Fill all the chinks and holes with snow and then cover the whole structure with a few inches of loose snow. In the event of very strong winds, it is also a good idea to build a small sheltering wall, or windbreak, to prevent the igloo becoming eroded by the wind or drifted over.

Once inside, you can go ahead and luxuriate building sleeping benches, and shelves, just like in the snow cave.

SNOW TRENCHES

In real emergency, when you need to get out of the wind fast, why not try a snow trench. This can be excavated with boots, ice axes, and the forebody or 'shovel' of the ski. It needs to be fairly narrow and about two metres long for two people, or longer, depending on how many are in the party. If possible, and in emergencies, build a roof of interwoven tree branches, but a tent or bivvy bag resting on your skis or ice axes does the same job better and quicker. Finally, cover the top over with snow for insulation. This provides a very crude, not very warm, but quick form of snow shelter.

In a similar vein, but slower, is the snow mound shelter. This is made by heaping lots and lots of soft snow into a mound, approximately six feet high and about ten feet in diameter. Once your mound is built, you must leave it for at least an hour for the snow to consolidate. We are working on the principle of age hardening, for snow when disturbed in this way, will consolidate and harden. Once the snow has consolidated, dig into it and carve out a living space, leaving a door and an air vent. The snow mound isn't as quick to build as the snow trench, but it is more comfortable to live in.

LIVING IN THE SNOW. POINTS TO REMEMBER.

1. The only way you will remain warm during the night is by sleeping in a dry sleeping bag, in dry clothes. Once your clothes or bag become wet, there is every chance that they will freeze. Once you are inside the shelter, strip off your wet clothes and stick them in a 'poly' bag or stuff sack and get inside your sleeping bag.
2. Digging a snow shelter is hard work and you will sweat heavily. So before you begin digging, strip off to the very minimum you will need for protection, so that the minimum of clothing will become wet from perspiration. Your windproof cagoule over a shirt should be protection enough while you are digging.
3. Make sure you have adequate ventilation. Failure to do this could result in DEATH from anoxia — which is simply lack of oxygen.
4. Bring all your gear inside the snow hole with you, especially your digging implements. The shelter may drift over and you will want to get

out again. When away from the snow hole, mark it well, and leave the digging implements outside. You may have to dig *in* again.

5. Bring boots and clothing up on the sleeping bench beside you, in a 'poly' bag and use them as a pillow. Do not leave them on the floor of the snow hole.
6. As in a tent, brush off all the snow from your clothing before you enter the shelter. If you don't, it will melt once you hit the warmer temperature inside the shelter and wet your clothes.
7. Avoid food which takes a lot of simmering or boiling. Water vapour given off from the pot will cause condensation to form and will dampen your sleeping bag and clothes.
8. A candle in the snow hole is well worth it for the cheeriness it gives. One single candle can illuminate even a large cave, for the snow reflects the light in a way I can only describe as being like Father Christmas's Grotto.
9. Put plenty of insulation between the snow and your sleeping bag. Don't lie directly on top of a 'poly' bag or plastic bivvy bag or you will slip off in the night.
10. Always leave a light burning if you have to get out of the shelter during the night. It may be the only way you'll find your way back. It is also a good idea to mark the outside top of the cave or snowhole, with some form of marker even in daytime.

10 · Winter Hazards

There is nothing inherently dangerous about camping in winter, providing that the camper is knowledgeable enough to cope with the problems which arise. It is true that the little difficulties which can arise are quite likely to be exacerbated by the conditions of winter, and this is something which the winter traveller has to watch out for continually. Tiredness at the end of a damp punishing day due to fighting a cold blustery wind, poor judgement thanks to the combined effects of cold and wet, all are symptoms of imminent danger.

It is when you are tired that mistakes can happen, usually just when the weather has decided to turn foul. We all make mistakes at some time or other, so there is no point in saying that the best cure is not to make mistakes in the first place. Let us think negatively, for a change and have a look at what to do if things do go wrong.

SLIPS

Statistically, slips are the major cause of most winter mountain accidents. We have discussed the ice axe and how to use it to brake when in a slip or slide, but this is a defensive action. Great care should be taken to prevent a slip occurring in the first place. Firstly, keep your footwear in good condition and replace worn or smooth soles and heels. Never tackle ground which may be too steep for you, especially under ice. Avoid icy slopes unless you are wearing crampons and have the necessary knowledge and experience to use them properly. Too many people think that cramponing is a completely natural activity, but it is not; it takes practice. A slide wearing crampons can be a nasty experience as the first reaction will be to drop the feet on the snow. The crampons will then dig in and act as a brake and the body will go head over heels so that you are now sliding down head first. Keep the cramponed feet in the air when sliding.

Practice ice axe braking at every opportunity. This is another skill which is severely under-practiced. It takes skill and lots of practice to become proficient at ice axe braking, and only by practice, practice, and more practice can you become expert at it. Remember too, to practice braking while *wearing a pack.* Too many people do their ice axe braking without realising that it will be much more difficult wearing a pack.

I have seen plenty of walkers climbing slopes with their ice axes still strapped to their packs. If the axe is on your pack you may as well not have one. Get it out at the first sign of snow, even on little slopes. Then you will have it handy and you will not be tempted to negotiate the steeper slopes without it.

A slip on snow covered ground doesn't always mean a long slide down the mountain. A slip on an ice covered rock can easily mean a twisted or broken ankle, so be extra careful on rough ground. It isn't very enjoyable wearing crampons on mixed ground of rock and ice, but you will have to weigh up the chances of a slip on ice which could result in injury, and if you consider this likely, stick with the crampons, even on the rock. I would urge

WIND CHILL

WIND CHILL CHART

Wind Speed	Local Temperature (F)			
0	32	23	14	5
5	29	20	10	1
10	18	7	−4	−15
15	13	−1	−13	−25
20	7	−6	−19	−32
30	1	−13	−27	−41

you to keep off any slope in winter which is too steep to negotiate without the use of a rope.

WINDCHILL

The big danger to the winter camper and traveller is the wind. A glance at the accompanying windchill chart shows how this works. Small amounts of air movements have considerable chilling effects because they carry away the thin layer of warm air which builds up near the body. Increasing wind speeds up to 40 mph have the effect of lowering the temperature and although after this speed there is little additional effect, you will by then have had enough. Low temperatures themselves are no real problem if you are *adequately clad and keep moving,* but if the wind rises then the *effective* temperature is much lower than the *true* air temperature. For example, at an actual thermometer reading of 5°F with a wind speed of 10 mph, the effective temperature drops to – 15°F, a temperature almost cold enough to freeze exposed flesh. If you are not prepared for winter winds then beware, they can be lethal, and always remember the windchill factor. Have windproof clothing, use a lip salve and barrier cream on the face and keep the head, ears and hands covered.

EXPOSURE (HYPOTHERMIA)

Exposure, or as it is more correctly known, hypothermia, is often found in wet-cold conditions. When the body becomes chilled, it begins to reduce circulation to the skin and to the extremities in order to maintain the proper temperature in the vital organs. This middle part of the body, the *inner core,* must be kept at a steady temperature. In normal conditions, the inner core remains at a constant 98.4°F and the preservation of this inner core temperature is vital. A fall in this core temperature leads to mental deterioration, loss of muscular control, eventual unconsciousness, and then death.

A fair definition of exposure would be: *"Severe chilling of the body surface leading to a progressive fall in body core temperature with the risk of death by hypothermia".*

People die from exposure in places other than mountains. Old folk often succumb to the winter cold in under-heated houses, and immersion in cold water leads to a quick cooling of the inner core resulting too often in death by hypothermia. In the mountains, cold alone rarely kills, but when cold is coupled with depleted energy reserves, or simple tiredness, the body can no longer keep a stable temperature and exposure can follow. It is essential to preserve a sufficient reserve of energy in severe conditions of high winds, cold and wet.

Wet weather plays a big part in many exposure cases. The cold rain, or snow soaks the walker's clothing, and greatly reduces the insulation against cold and wind, leaving him open to conditions which otherwise would have been easily avoided. Early use of the shell clothing is the best defence here.

Over-estimation of fitness and under-estimation of the time needed to reach your destination are common subsidiary causes of exposure. Inadequate diet is another. The human body is like a machine and constantly needs fuel to keep it going. The harder you push your body, the more fuel you need, and on a hard winter hike your energy needs could rise to 4,000 calories or more per day. Your kit should contain a high energy snack lunch to be eaten on the trail. So, to prevent hypothermia, eat well, have the proper clothing, avoid chilling from wind or wet, and don't attempt too much in adverse conditions.

SYMPTOMS

It is not always easy to decide when you have a case of exposure on your hands. It is even more difficult to realise when you yourself are becoming a victim, which is another reason for not travelling alone on winter treks. Watch your companions, and make sure that they are constantly keeping a check on you. If you suspect the early symptoms of exposure you may be able to avoid a crisis by early treatment.

A person beginning to suffer from hypothermia will generally be awkward, both in his movements and attitude. Unreasonable behaviour and complaints of coldness and fatigue may be signs that exposure is taking effect. The victim may start shivering, stumble, speak with a slurred voice, have sudden, violent outbursts of energy, and may react aggressively to suggestions that he stops walking and takes shelter. It should be emphasised that under difficult conditions members of a party should keep close together and watch each other carefully. Always be alert to this situation.

TREATMENT

As soon as the symptoms are established, stop. If the victim has collapsed and become unconscious, send for help, for the situation is grave. Maintaining the temperature of the inner core is vital. Bearing this in mind it is folly to cause the blood to circulate in the extremeties of the body surface by rubbing, or adding surface warmth, such as hot water bottles (even if you had them) or alcohol. The inner core needs the blood circulating down there. The first thing must be to insulate the victim from the elements and use every means possible to keep his inner core temperature stable. Then re-warm the victim. If he is wet, remove the wet clothes, dry him and put him into a pre-warmed sleeping bag. Pitch the tent for shelter. A freshly unpacked sleeping bag isn't much good, as the victim will probably not have enough heat output to warm it up, so put a fit companion inside the sleeping bag also to give added body warmth. Pay particular attention to the ground insulation. Make sure there is a windproof and waterproof covering around the bag, either in a tent or a survival bag. If he can take food, limit it to sweet, warm, but not too hot drinks, given in small swallows. Do not force alcohol into an unconscious person. The blood supply to the stomach at this stage is so limited that heavy foods will not be digested. If respiration stops, perform mouth-to-mouth resuscitation. Keep the victim warm until help arrives, even if he apparently recovers and insists on carrying on. (See the Venture Guide to *Outdoor First Aid*).

FROSTNIP

The first stage of frostbite, or first degree frostbite, is known as *frostnip.* This is not too serious, but it is alarming and serves as a warning of worse things to follow. Frostnip is the freezing of the outer layers of skin tissue. Firstly, the affected part will feel burningly cold, and then it will go numb. If this happens, true frostbite has developed. The skin will take on a bleached appearance and the surface will feel cold and hard to the touch. By pressing, you may feel the layers of tissue below, still soft and resilient. Frostnip can be dealt with straight away by warming. If it is a finger, stick it into your armpit. Toes require more attention, chafing or pressing them to warm on your partner's stomach. A painful, prickling sensation will occur as the nipped area rewarms. The skin may appear mottled and bleached for some time, and it is important that the part, once affected, should be well protected from further freezing. The skin may later split and peel, rather like sunburn.

FROSTBITE

Frostbite and exposure are closely related. One of the body's first reactions to severe chill is to cut off the circulation to the extremities, in order to preserve heat at the body core. This reduces the blood supply to toes, fingers and the other extremities and provides ready access for frostbite. Frostbite problems usually occur when temperatures are abnormally low, or when someone gets wet or is forced to bivouac in very bad weather.

Frostbite is an injury resulting from freezing of the tissues, which usually occurs in the hands, feet, or face, but can occur elsewhere. It is easily avoided with reasonable care. In addition to the maintenance of general body warmth, pay careful attention to the state of your hands and feet. Tight fitting clothing or tight boot lacing which cuts circulation should be avoided. Tight pack straps are another contributing factor. Painfully cold feet or hands which *suddenly cease to hurt* should be taken care of immediately, but it is better to keep them warm, even though it means taking off gaiters, boots and socks. If the warning signs are ignored, a long and painful process of frostbite may well occur with the possibility of tissue loss and crippled limbs.

TREATMENT

Prevention is better than cure, so avoid tight boots and clothing which restrict circulation, and keep the extremities warm.

Should frostbite really set in, the affected part will appear white and will feel like cold stone. If the freezing continues the part will go numb, but may then feel warm. This warmth is an illusion, and indicates a very serious stage of frostbite and tissue injury is inevitable. If at all possible, the victim should be taken to medical help. If it is the feet which are frozen, then he should be treated as a stretcher case. Never expect someone with frostbitten feet to walk unless it is absolutely necessary. Although it may be possible to walk on frozen feet, it will be impossible to walk once they have been re-warmed, when the pain is severe. Do not, under any circumstances, rub the affected part with snow. It will only do further damage.

The frozen part must be thawed out all at once, rather than gradually, and preferably under medical supervision. Heat some water until it is tepid, about 108°F. If you don't have a thermometer test the water by dipping your elbow in it. It should feel pleasantly warm. Keeping the water at that temperature, soak the part for twenty to thirty minutes. Don't be tempted to massage the affected part, break any blisters which have formed, or exercise the limb. As soon as possible, get the victim to hospital, making sure that the injured part is well protected.

CONCLUSIONS

Exposure and frostbite are particularly dangerous conditions, but don't let that put you off winter camping. A well equipped and knowledgeable outdoors person (which we assume you are) will recognise the signs and symptoms well in advance and will take the necessary action. If you are careful these emergencies will never occur in the first place, and don't think that because your hands become a little cold that frostbite is around the corner. On the other hand, never become too complacent. It can happen to you and it is always better to be on the safe side.

SNOWBLINDNESS

This is a very painful condition brought about by exposure to intense ultra-violet radiation. You have, in effect, got sunburned eyeballs and this is just as painful as it sounds. As snow reflects about 90 per cent of the sun's ultra violet light, it is not enough to protect the eyes from the direct glare of the sun. Snow goggles should be worn for these give all round protection.

The condition varies greatly in intensity, but the general symptoms are a severe headache with painful bloodshot eyes. Apart from pain killing drugs, not much can be done, so you will have to cover the eyes for a while and rest.

Eye protection is advisable, even on overcast days in the snowfields. When the weather is dull, the pupils dilate in response to the poor light, and so let in more radiation, so whenever the ground is completely covered in snow, wear goggles or sunglasses.

NAVIGATION

Winter certainly brings us beautiful days of clear pristine weather, but it can also bring a plentiful supply of misty, foggy, or snowy days, all of which make navigation that little bit more difficult. Snowfalls mean that many landmarks are covered over, including rivers and streams, so you must rely more on good compass work and map reading than ever before.

When the weather is good, navigation can be done quickly and effectively by map reading alone, but when conditions worsen, other skills become necessary. Good compass work, the ability to estimate time and distances, and maybe the use of an altimeter, are going to be required.

WHITEOUTS

A 'whiteout' is a situation which occurs in snow covered country when falling snow and mist become so dense that one cannot distinguish it from the ground, and visibility is reduced to almost zero. You will have to slow your pace to a crawl, use the compass to maintain direction, and beware of crevasses.

AVALANCHES

There are two main type of avalanche, the *loose snow* and the *slab.* These classifications are based on the snow state at the *origin* of the avalanche.

LOOSE SNOW AVALANCHES

Loose snow has poor adhesion qualities so that the crystals are held together by friction rather than by bonding.

An avalanche situation arises when snow accumulates on slopes at a steeper angle than its natural angle of repose. When the snow piles up beyond this angle, a few crystals can start moving, or be triggered, and a chain reaction then takes place. The snow moves downhill and then spreads laterally until more and more snow is collected into a sliding mass. Once gentler slopes are reached the pile loses its momentum and comes to rest. *Loose snow* avalanches normally occur when the snow is either very wet or very dry, and they are therefore common during and after a fresh fall of snow in calm conditions and in Spring, when the snow becomes wet with melt water. Wet snow avalanches are heavier, slower and probably more dangerous. The *'airborne powder'* avalanche is the most explosive version of the type.

SLAB AVALANCHES

This is the most common type of avalanche, and the type which is responsible for the majority of winter accidents. These are more complex than the loose snow type, with a large area of snow breaking away from above and sliding at one time. The snow is cohesive to a certain extent and has previously been anchored to the slope and comes away as a solid slab.

Obviously, the weight of the slab can be no greater than the strength of its anchorage, and whenever stress exceeds the strength of the anchorage, the slab will crack and begin to slide. This breaking away can be caused by many factors such as temperature changes, wind, or not infrequently, the weight of skiers or walkers.

SOFT SLAB AVALANCHES

These are most likely to happen after and during snow storms. The danger may last for several days if the weather is cold. The *soft slab* avalanche is often associated with high winds, when the lee slopes become particularly prone to avalanching. The characteristics include a distinct fracture line, a silent break which can take you completely by surprise. The soft slab breaks up while it is flowing and leaves very few distinct blocks, or slabs of snow in the debris.

Danger signs include a rapid accumulation of snow, such as a very heavy snow fall. It is advisable to treat all major winter storms as a source of soft slab danger. Storms which start cold and finish warm are more likely to produce avalanche conditions than the reverse. If you find yourself setting off tiny soft snow slides from your boots or skis on easy terrain, it is a fair certainty that a hazard exists at higher elevations, or on steeper ground, so stay away until the situation stabilises.

HARD SLAB

This is one of the most dangerous of avalanche risks as the hardness of the snow can lead you into a false sense of security. This type of danger is very hard to recognise. Hard slabs are generally confined to lee slopes and are usually formed at low temperatures, so treat cold and windy weather with the greatest suspicion when using high slabbed slopes. When travelling over hard packed snow treat any hollow rumbling sounds as warnings of unstable slab. Hard wind slab usually has a chalky non-reflective appearance, but don't put too much emphasis on this as the slab itself could very well be hidden under fresh snowfalls.

Hard slab avalanches fracture in much the same way as soft slab, but usually release with a loud crack. The slabs do not break up as finely as soft slab, but will leave large blocks in the debris.

CLIMAX AVALANCHES

This type is formed by a build-up of snow on top of a deep-seated layer in the snow cover, usually depth hoar. It is often associated with a prolonged early cold spell. Unless you know the snow history of the area for the entire winter, it is really very difficult to guess when a climax avalanche will take place. Fortunately this type of fall is very rare, and does not really constitute a great hazard for the walker or skier, but it is good to remember that in avalanche detection you can never tell what will happen next. Avalanches can happen anywhere you have snow.

WET SNOW AVALANCHE

Wet snow avalanches constitute the major avalanche hazard in spring time, when free water lubricates and weakens the bonding between layers. They do not occur at temperatures *below* freezing point. The avalanche can be of slab formation, or the loose snow type, starting from a fracture line across the slope, or from a single point, depending on the snow conditions, but the primary cause is rain soaking the snow cover.

Another cause is sudden warm and overcast weather which causes the snow to melt and become heavy with water. Although these avalanches move more slowly than other types, because of the heavy weight of the water laden snow, they can be very destructive. Danger signs include wet sticky snow, cracks and rifts in the snow cover, and large snowballs. Early afternoon in fair weather is the critical time.

AVALANCHE SLOPES

Snow has elastic and viscous qualities. The higher the temperature of the snow, the higher the viscosity. Conversely the colder it is the more brittle the snow mass may become. On a flat surface, snow will settle quite substantially under the stresses of further falls, *destructive metamorphism* and gravity. On a slope, gravity is always pulling the snow mass downhill. This settling action causes an imperceptible 'creep' down the hill, producing forces and stresses within the snow. On a convex slope, the snow becomes greatly stretched, while on the concave part of the slope the snow becomes compressed. It is on the convex slopes that the avalanche danger becomes apparent. The top part of the snow cover tries to pull away and it is here that we could expect avalanche trigger points, or fracture lines for slab avalanches.

The conclusion which can be drawn from this phenomena is that the warmer the snow, the greater the elasticity and its ability to conform and

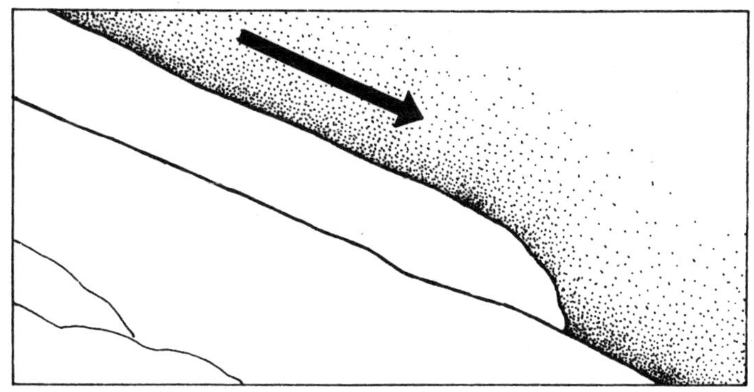

FLOWING AVALANCHE

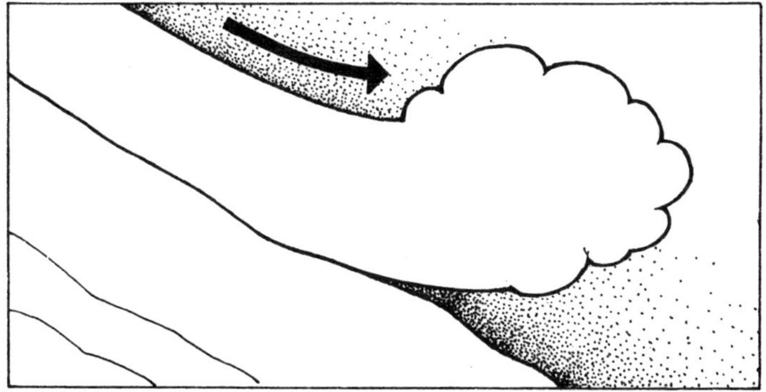

AIRBORNE POWDER AVALANCHE

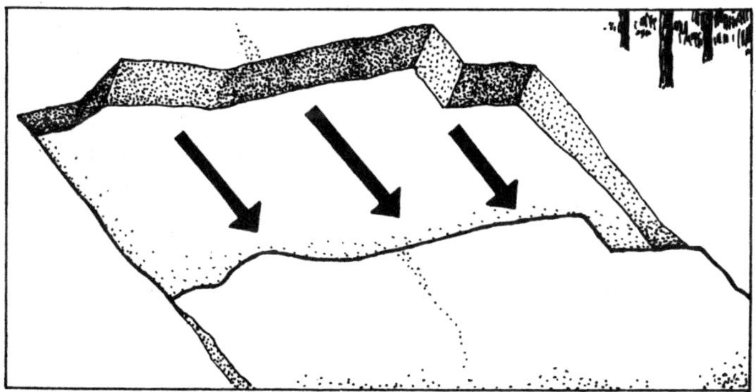

SLAB AVALANCHE

adjust to these stresses. In colder temperatures, the snow is slower to adjust to stresses and tension builds up, which if not released artificially by avalanche teams or by avalanching itself, persists for longer periods. So, after storms or temperature changes the snow may quickly stabilise, but the avalanche risk may linger on for a considerable time.

CORNICES

It would be wrong to finish talking about avalanche types without mentioning cornices. These very beautiful waves of overhanging snow build up on the lee side of ridges, or on the top of escarpments. Unfortunately they can be as dangerous as they are beautiful. Collapsing cornices are common triggers of slab avalanches on the slopes below. Do not walk up on to cornices and stay away from corniced escarpments. If the cornice fractures it will carry away at a point well *behind* the crest and can take you with it.

AVALANCHE PROTECTION

Obviously the best way to avoid an avalanche is to avoid a snow covered mountain, but once you commit yourself to the hills as a winter walker or camper then that option is no longer open, so you must learn as much about avalanche protection as possible. Find out as much as you can about the snow history of the area; familiarise yourself with different snow conditions. Avoid dangerous slopes and obvious avalanche paths like the plague, and if you really must cross a dangerous area, only expose one member of the party at a time. If one man is buried then his chances of rescue are good, if his companions are able to help him and act quickly.

Finally — NEVER GO ALONE.

Despite these words of caution, people will continue to be caught in avalanches, so don't say, *"It will never happen to me"*. If you are caught, remember the following procedure . . . as you go under:-

1. Call out so that others can follow your course and see where you disappear in case you are buried.
2. Get rid of ski poles, skis, rucksack or ice axe. The snow will twist them and fracture your bones.
3. Attempt a *swimming* or *rolling* motion to stay on the surface or at the front of the slide. You will probably find this a natural reaction, but whatever happens, do your utmost to stay above the surface and try and work your way to the front or to one side of the avalanche.
4. If you find yourself going under and your attempts at keeping above the surface are to no avail, cover your face with your hands. This will help to keep snow out of your nose and mouth. Clear a breathing space in front of your mouth and chest as you stop. Avalanche snow becomes very, very hard almost as soon as it stops moving. Having your hands near your face will help to clear some head room before the snow really cakes.
5. Do not panic. Easier said than done, I admit, but frantic efforts to free yourself will only use up precious energy and oxygen. Do not shout — no one can hear you.
6. If you have a chance to dig yourself out, make sure you are digging the correct way. People have been known to become disorientated and dig themselves deeper in. Trickle some salive on to your lips and note which way it runs; then dig in the *opposite* direction.

7. If you hear a rescue party above do not waste valuable energy and air by shouting to them; they won't hear you. Sound is transmitted into the snow quite well, but it is transmitted out very poorly.

COURSE OF RESCUE

If it is your companion who is caught, and the avalanche misses you, you are immediately involved in a rescue situation. Act as follows:-

1. Do not panic.
2. Mark the point where your friend was last seen. This will greatly reduce the area to be searched, which will be *below* this point.
3. Before going for help, it is very important that you first make a careful search of the area. If possible, leaving one person searching while you go for help, but have a quick search anyway even if you are the sole survivor. Speed is essential in avalanche rescue.
4. If the initial search fails, start probing the snow surface with an ice axe or ski pole or whatever else is available. Your friend may be buried well below the surface, but if you are alone you should carefully decide when to break off the search and go for help. The proximity of the rescue post will be the deciding factor. If there are several survivors, send two for help, while the others keep searching. If it will take more than two hours for help to reach the scene, the victim may well have a better chance if everyone stays and searches. Again, weigh up the circumstances carefully.
5. When and if you do go for help, be very, very careful. Avoid any more avalanche dangers and injuries from trying to move too fast. Mark the accident scene on your map and take a note of the grid reference. Avoid exhausting yourself on the way out as you will have to lead the rescue team back to the scene.
6. If you are lucky and the victim is found, treat him immediately for suffocation and shock. Free his nose and mouth of snow and administer artifical resuscitation. Keep the victim as dry as possible, remove any snow from inside his clothing and put him in a sleeping bag with his head downhill. Use your knowledge of First Aid to treat any other injuries.

AVOIDING AVALANCHES

Safety teams and forecasters in all the major mountain areas in the world give ample warning of avalanche risk. Before you head off on your trip, check with Mountain Rescue stations, ski patrols, and Forest Ranger offices, or National Park wardens, on the avalanche risk in their areas.

Be wary of the following types of terrain:-

1. Gullies and open areas in forests. Dense timber may protect you but a few scattered trees on an otherwise open slope will not offer very much protection.
2. Open bare slopes, sloped between 30° and 45°. On slopes like this the avalanche risk is greatest.
3. The lee sides of high steep ridges or corries (cirques).
4. Underneath obvious cornices.

If your route unavoidable runs across an obvious path, then you have several options:-

1. If possible, circle it at the top. It is usually more practical to bypass the run-out at the bottom by taking a detour wide enough to avoid the avalanche run-out.
2. Stick to ridge crests where possible when ascending and descending slopes.
3. If there seems to be no way round the avalanche path, consider the possibilities of an avalanche occurring. Ask yourself if it is avalanche weather, has it been snowing or very windy? Has the temperature risen?

You should learn as much about avalanche theory as possible for it is your finest protection.

AVALANCHE CORDS OR SONDE

A useful safety device is the simple avalanche, or *oertal* cord, a 100ft (33 metre) length of brightly coloured red cord marked with small arrows. You can simply attach one end to your belt with the arrows pointing towards you and trail the cord behind you. Then, in case of a burial this cord should float to the surface and your companions can trace you quickly. The *Pieps* sonde, a small transmitter, is another popular avalanche precaution and may be hired from many outdoor shops. This gives out a 'bleep' and your position can be quickly located should you be buried by an avalanche.

Finally, if you *must* cross avalanche paths, remember to only expose one member of the party at a time. If you hear cracking or creaking noises, or perhaps see cracks shooting out in front of you, retreat immediately, as carefully as speed will allow. Most avalanche victims trigger off the avalanche themselves.

THE MOUNTAIN CODE

Every snow camper should know and employ the Mountain Code:-

1. Select equipment only after asking advice and then learn how to use it.
2. Have a knowledge of First Aid.
3. Know how to navigate properly, with map and compass.
4. Attain a standard of physical fitness suited to your ambition.
5. Follow the Country Code.
6. Always carry: Waterproofs; spare sweater; map; compass; whistle; emergency food with chocolate or sugar; a First Aid Kit; a polythene survival bag for emergencies. In winter increase clothing and food and carry a good torch with spare batteries and bulb, plus mitts and balaclava.
7. Never go alone.
8. Check the local weather forecast before you leave your base.
9. Only venture on to snow and ice when you have fully mastered the techniques of ice axe and crampons.
10. In the event of injury, carry out immediate first-aid, evacuate the casualty or erect a shelter. Signal your distress. Other walkers may be near by and able to assist you, or telephone the police and ask for Mountain Rescue. The International Mountain Distress Signal is six rapid signals or blasts on a whistle repeated at one minute intervals until you are located.
11. Conditions can change rapidly, so be prepared to turn back if the weather deteriorates. High winds and icing can be serious hazards.

12. Low cloud and mist can slow up most parties. Exercise caution. Walk at a speed which gives a good view of the immediate ground ahead.
13. After heay rain or severe thawing the crossing of rivers by stepping stones or low bridges may be impossible. Do not attempt unorthodox crossings unless they are well practised. Travel up or down stream to a safe crossing point.
14. Summer and winter weather conditions pose their own problems. Know the symptoms and treatment of heat exhaustion and exposure.
15. Expeditions to high mountains and roped rock climbing require special skills and winter mountaineering can be a most serious undertaking. An understanding of the hazards posed by cornices and avalanche prone slopes is absolutely necessary. Daylight hours are less in winter and conditions far harsher, and should be considered accordingly.

If you know *and apply* this Code you will not come to much harm.

NOW GET OUT THERE AND DO IT

It is important not to be discouraged by all the skills and knowledge necessary for safe snow camping. Many of the skills are fun to learn, and much of the knowledge necessary is fascinating to acquire. Once you have become familiar with all hints and tips, the skills and knowledge, the outdoor world is your oyster, and no more will you have to pack everything away in October and curse the bad weather of winter until spring comes round again. The snow camper is the complete camper, snug and secure in comfort and knowledge that few people can understand. *"You must be mad to live in a tiny tent out there in the snow",* becomes a common comment from non-understanding friends. It isn't a question of toughness, but of understanding the winter world and appreciating that you can live happily in a hard environment, with a minimum of the luxuries which so many take for granted.

Snow camping and winter backpacking are not exactly normal activities. It takes a special attitude to enjoy living in the snow. Not everyone who reads this book will go on to become a contented, converted, snow camper. Some may be just unhappy in the cold, in the same way that many are unhappy in intense heat, but I believe that if you have the interest to pick up this book and read it, and hopefully learn from it, then the motivation will be supplied by that first glance outside your tent on a snow covered morning, with the sun just appearing and causing the crystals to sparkle — but I think this is where I came in . . .

Bibliography

All snow campers should study the following books.

Mountaineering — Alan Blackshaw — Penguin Books U.K.
Mountain Leadership — Eric Langmuir (Scottish Sports Council) U.K.
Mountain Weather for Climbers — David Unwin — Cordee. U.K.
Mountain Navigation — Peter Cliff. U.K.
Mountain and Cave Rescue. Mountain Rescue Committee. U.K.
Avalanches and Snow Safety — Colin Fraser — John Murray. U.K.
ABC of Avalanche Safety — La Chappelle. U.S.A.
Avalanche Handbook — Agriculture Dept. U.S.A.
Spur Book of Winter Camping — Terry Brown & Rob Hunter — Spurbooks U.K.
Spur Book of Backpacking — Robin Adshead (2nd Ed.) — Spurbooks. U.K.
Spur Book of Cross Country Skiing — Rob Hunter — Spurbooks. U.K.
Walking Softly in the Wilderness — Sierra Club. U.S.A.
Backpacking in Britain — Robin Adshead — Oxford Illustrated Press. U.K.
The Photoguide to Mountains for Backpackers and Climbers — Douglas Milner.
Mountaineering in Scotland — Bill Murray — Diadem Books
Undiscovered Scotland — Bill Murray — Diadem Books
Wilderness Skiing — Tejado-Flores — Sierra Club. U.S.A.
Nordic Touring and Cross Country Skiing — Brady
Snow and Ice Techniques — Bill March — Cicerone Press. U.K.
Ski Touring — Rob Hunter — Spurbooks U.K.
Outdoor Companion — Rob Hunter — Constable. U.K.
Outdoor First Aid — Rob Hunter & Terry Brown — Spurbooks. U.K.

The following magazines often contain useful articles on Snow Camping:

Climber & Rambler (U.K.)
Practical Camper (U.K.)
Backpacker Magazine (U.S.A.)
The Great Outdoors (U.K.)
Outdor Canada (Canada)
Mariah (U.S.A.)
Camping (UK)